The

IMMUNE SYSTEM

of the

SOUL

The Journey from Awareness to
Realization to Transformation

Mike George

The Immune System of the Soul
The Journey from Awareness to Realization to Transformation

Mike George

Text Copyright Mike George 2013

Print Edition ISBN: 978-0-9576673-0-3

Also available
Kindle Edition ISBN: 978-0-9576673-1-0
Epub Edition ISBN: 978-0-9576673-2-7

First published by Gavisus Media 2013
St Peters Cottages, Broad Hinton, Wiltshire SN4 9PA
Email: gavisusmedia@gmail.com

The moral rights of the author have been asserted.

Cover Design: Antoneta Wotringer
Designer: Charlotte Mouncey www.bookstyle.co.uk

The information given in this book should not be treated as a substitute for professional medical advice; always consult a medical practitioner. Any use of information in this book is at the reader's discretion and risk. Neither the author nor the publisher can be held responsible for any loss, claim or damage arising out of use, or misuse, or the suggestions made or the failure to take medical advice.

Also by Mike George

The 7 Myths About LOVE...Actually!
The Journey from Your Head to the Heart of Your Soul

Don't Get MAD Get Wise
Why no one ever makes you angry...ever!

The 7 AHA!s of Highly Enlightened Souls
How to Free YOUR Self from ALL Forms of Stress

Learn to Find Inner Peace
Discover the true self, manage anxieties and emotions, think well, feel well

Learn to Relax
Ease tension, conquer stress and free the self

In the Light of Meditation
A guide to meditation and spiritual development

1001 Ways to Relax
Beat stress and find perfect calm, anywhere, anytime

1001 Meditations
Discover peace of mind

Subscribe to Clear Thinking

Clear Thinking is a regular e-article (once or twice a month) that Mike currently circulates to around 15,000 people worldwide. Topics vary, but they all serve to sustain the ongoing learning and unlearning that is required to restore your awareness of your true self.

If you would like to subscribe, go to www.relax7.com or send an email to mike@relax7.com - it's free.

Contents

PART THREE
BE Well - STAY Well - GO Well

Being UNWELL

When you are an 'unwell being' you will likely feel closed and isolated, sometimes aggrieved and victimized, perhaps anxious and apprehensive, often melancholic and depressed or just frustrated and extremely stressed! In other words, you will create and feel a combination of emotions, all adaptations of the three families of emotion that signal unwellness - sadness, anger and fear. It's likely the world will appear to be a somewhat forbidding and unfriendly place. Other people will often need to be tolerated! You will probably look back frequently at what seemed to be better days. And whenever you look forwards there seems to be little light at the end of the tunnel.

Being unwell however, is generally considered to be 'normal'. Listen to many cappuccino conversations and you will notice how unwellness easily becomes a perverted form of comfort!

Being WELL

When you are a 'well being' you are open and warmly willing to connect with almost anyone. There will be an effortless enthusiasm, a cheerful and sunny demeanour, that pulls others into your aura. Even when difficult circumstances come to call you are unphased and able to meet them with an easiness that affirms your mastery of your own thoughts and feelings. Your heart is ever-ready to lovingly meet the needs of others. You can easily forget the trials and tribulations of yesteryear as you cruise happily into a bright, brand new tomorrow.

Being well can seem abnormal to some and positively irritating to many of the unwell! So it is, that a 'well being' in the modern world, sometimes seems out of place!

I AM

Unwellness is popular, not by common consent, but by an all pervasive ignorance that has one deep, hidden, ancient, root cause. Unwellness is a sign that you have learned to believe you are someone other than who you really are! Wellness cannot be restored until you know your self as nothing more than the 'I' that says, "I am".

If you put anything after 'I am' it is not you. It's a fiction, a construct, a figment of your imagination! As a consequence you will suffer, but it's unlikely you will make the connection. When you believe that you are more than just the 'I' that says, "I am," you unknowingly diminish your self and sabotage your peaceful and loving nature!

You start to believe that you have 'to go and be' somewhere else, that you have 'to go and do' something important, that you have 'to go and achieve' something significant. All of which results in a kind of perpetual absence from your own life.

These are the strategies that we use to avoid being our self. Hence the saying, "Someone who is trying to be somebody doesn't know how to be!"

To be or not to be, is always false choice!

You always are the 'I' that says, "I am."

And that's ALL...you are!

PART ONE

Are YOU a Well Being?

disease
A pathological condition of a part, organ, or system of an organism resulting from various causes, such as infection or genetic defect or stress, and characterized by an identifiable group of signs or symptoms.

dis - ease
A condition of consciousness that arises due to a loss of self-awareness and the attachment to, and identification with, a mental image/idea, characterized by an identifiable group of specific types of thoughts and emotions.

The difference between Health and Wellbeing

We are probably living in the most health-conscious era in history. We can become an expert on almost any disease in a matter of hours. With two clicks of a mouse, we can summon the international consultant and guru of all health issues, otherwise known as Google, and have instant access to the symptoms, causes and cures of a thousand ailments.

But none of them can tell us why we are all not well!

If you tap into your search engine the vaguest description of a lump, an ache or an itch, you will be flooded by a river of information and an unlimited supply of diagnostic insights. You will be granted access to the understandings of both mainstream treatments and 'alternative wisdoms' through hundreds of links in a hundred countries. How did our parents survive without it? In reality, extremely well!

The health of our body is no longer just an occasional conversation for a few. It is now an obsessional pre-occupation for many. But the real question today is not how healthy can your body be, but are YOU a well being? Health and well-being, while obviously connected, are two different things.

Good health refers to the form that we occupy, but 'well being' refers to ... well, your being! You could have a healthy body but not be well in your being. Over time however, the unwellness of your being will likely translate into deteriorating health of the form that you occupy! You could be a well being while your body could be a catalogue of different ailments. Yet, we now know that if you maintain your wellbeing it will more than likely have an efficacious effect on your body's health and even empower the healing of many of those ailments.

Our wellbeing is primary and the physical health of our body is secondary. However, because we know so little about what it means to 'be well' and how to 'stay well' in our being, we make our physical health primary and almost ignore the wellness of our being.

Science is silent about being!

In the age of the medical expert, it's easy to detect, define and describe both a state of 'good health' and the various conditions of 'ill health'. As our body is both visible and tangible it's easy to work out the what, why and how things go wrong. But it's obviously not so easy to see and understand why we are not well in our being. With physical disease we have scientific procedures and ways to measure, understand and heal almost any ailment. But 'wellness of being' is not measurable, simply because you can't get a 'being' into a test tube! Being cannot be subjected to a scalpel. This basically means 'science' has nothing to say about wellness, because science has no way of measuring the wellness of our being, never mind why and how we 'beings' become unwell.

That's probably why science in general, and medical science in particular, resists the idea that the deterioration and absence of well being is such a major factor in physical disease. However, as modern technology facilitates the instant sharing of insights into mental and spiritual wellness, and as we increase our personal understanding of our states of being, it seems more of us are learning how to gauge more accurately how well we really are...in our being! Gradually, an increasing number of people have grown both wiser and more intuitively aware of the direct link between the wellness of their being and the health of their body. While we can all benefit from such wisdom, there is still no substitute for turning our attention inwards and seeing for our self.

Measuring Up!

There are many ways to assess and evaluate the wellness of your being. Wellness is defined not by measurable 'quantities' but by the 'quality' of your thoughts and attitudes, the levels of your happiness and contentment, the consistency of your capacity to lovingly and compassionately connect with others, the stability of your feelings and the extent to which you feel that you are the master of the choices that you make. In this regard, you are your own scientist and the laboratory is your own consciousness. The tests you run all require the instrument of your own awareness, as you observe and measure the clarity of your perceptions, the quality of your thoughts and feelings, and the benevolence of your intentions.

Being able to see and identify the causes of any loss of wellbeing and know the ways to restore our being to wellness, are the primary abilities of someone who is able to *be well* at will, *stay well* wherever they are, and *go well* through the challenges and tests that life presents us all each and every day.

The purpose of this little book is to understand a little more about the true nature of 'wellbeing', what we do to sabotage it, how to gain some measure of how well we are and finally how we reawaken our spiritual immune system in order to restore and maintain our wellness.

If anything is not clear, please do
make contact at mike@relax7.com

The Difference between Pain and Suffering

As the old saying goes 'pain is compulsory but suffering is optional'. Pain is what we will inevitably feel when something happens to the body that we occupy. But suffering is what we create at a mental and emotional level in 'response' to what happens to our body, and to what we perceive is happening in and to the world around us. Our body could be in pain, but we could choose not to suffer. Some do manage to make that choice. They accept that the physical pain is inevitable, but they don't dwell on it, they don't blame others for it, they don't worry about its duration, they don't suffer mentally or emotionally. They tend to accept the presence of the pain and just get on with life. Not easy for most of us, but it seems possible.

On the other hand, while most people's physical health is fine, they might spend their life suffering as they judge, blame, criticize and condemn others and/or rage against events in the world. Woven through those, and many other 'behaviors', are the emotions of suffering.

Pain is physical and suffering is mental/emotional. Pain is a signal that your body sends to your brain. The message is you need to change something within the energies of your physical form. It obviously means something needs to be healed. Suffering is an emotional message that says you have lost control of your perceptions, thoughts and feelings, and if you want to not suffer you need to change the way you 'perceive and think' about what is going on around you.

Pain can be caused by another person if they do something to your body, but suffering is always caused by one's self according to what you believe, which then shapes how and what you perceive. That's why one person looks out from their prison cell and sees only the bars, while the guy in the next cell looks out and sees only the stars! Suffering can always be a choice. That's not easy to see in a world that generally runs on the belief that we suffer naturally at the hands of our parents, managers, governments and even our weather! It's a sign that we have forgotten that no one else is responsible for our thoughts and the emotions that we create and feel. That one 'realization' alone, that *it's always me and not them who makes me think and feel this way*, is an insight that can ultimately allow you to free your self from all suffering. If you want to!

What's Natural?

Many of us have learned to believe that suffering is natural, that it's human nature, that it is what makes us human. Few of us question that particular belief. So we fail to see it for what it is - a false belief! If we believe that suffering is natural and therefore OK, then it's likely our suffering, which is code for 'unhappiness', will gradually increase in our life and we won't have realized we could have done something about it. But if you can realize all suffering is self-created, then you awaken to the possibility of eliminating the belief that you are a 'helpless victim'.

The realization that you are never a victim, if you so choose, can change almost everything from your day-to-day feelings to the quality of your entire life! However, to achieve that, you will need to check, challenge and change the many beliefs that you have inherited during childhood, absorbed in the process of your education and assimilated during your 'passage' into the world of so-called adults. It's those beliefs that subconsciously hold almost everyone's state of being to ransom as they become the seeds of extremely unatural and therefore unwell states of being.

The reflections within this book are intended to highlight the most common and most debilitating beliefs that cause us to suffer. That will allow you to see whether they are present within your consciousness and then to understand how those beliefs are like 'infections' that sabotage your wellness. Ultimate you may come to see that all your stress, all your sorrow and all your suffering have their roots in the beliefs that you consciously and subconsciously hold to be true.

There are also some precise insights, sprinkled with a little wisdom, as to how you can end your suffering and restore your being to a state of wellness, if you want to do that inner work. Many people don't want to end their suffering! They don't want to be well in their being. Strange as it may seem, many of us become attached to our unhappiness, comfortable with our resentments, satisfied with our stress! We can even use our emotional suffering to form the basis of our sense of who we are. When we use our discontentments in this way, it becomes similar to a physical disease that gets right into the bones and is therefore hard to shift. When our unhappiness seeps into our sense of identity, it can be hard to liberate our self from what might be diagnosed as a 'chronic condition of being' otherwise known as 'misidentification.' This is the ultimate root cause of all that ails our being and makes us unwell. While it's hard to discern it's also why, as you will discover, there is ultimately only one cure for all the various forms of human suffering. There are many treatments and cures for all our physical diseases but there is only one 'ultimate cure' for all our spiritual dis - eases!

That cure can be realised in an instant. More commonly, it takes time to emerge from deep within our soul. Only then can we restore complete immunity to all the various forms of spiritual dis - ease. Only then can we **be** well, **stay** well and **go** well again.

Understanding the Soul's Immune System

When any area of the cellular energy of our body is invaded by an 'energy form' that is of an unfriendly or incompatible nature, the 'helper cells' of the immune system, often referred to as antibodies and white blood cells, almost immediately detect the presence of the invader. They move quickly to the relevant location to protect the affected parts of our body. When they arrive, they are able to discern and distinguish the exact nature of the invasion and/or the precise nature of the deviation that happens to the body's own cells. Their work is to either extinguish, expel or encircle, and thereby contain what might be called 'cellular malfunctions', which we tend to call...disease!

While we may experience the pain of occasional disease in our body, we all suffer from many moments of dis - ease within our consciousness, within our being. Moments of dis - ease are signals that tell us that our wellbeing is being compromised. They can range from a quiet feeling of uneasiness at one end of the spectrum to states of extreme stress, that might include anything from deep sorrow to utter rage to abject terror, at the other end of the 'dis - ease spectrum'.

The purpose of the 'immune system of our body' is to detect and distinguish, protect and often extinguish from our body the many types of physical disease of which we are now mostly familiar. The 'immune system of the soul' works in a similar way on the many kinds of 'dis - ease' that occur within our consciousness, within our being. The first symptom of any loss of wellbeing, the first sign of any 'dis - ease' occurring within our consciousness, is usually a 'feeling' of mental or emotional uneasiness!

In the context of all the dis - eases of consciousness that we will explore together here, I use the words *self, soul, consciousness* and *being* synonymously. They all refer to the 'I' that says, "I am," as distinct from the body that we occupy. While the energy of the physical body is what we call 'matter', the energy of the soul/self is what we sometimes call 'spirit'. One is visible and tangible, and the other is invisible and intangible. Spirit is the being that I am/you are. Another way to say this in the context of this approach to the dis - eases of consciousness is that you don't have a soul, you are the soul. You don't have consciousness, you are consciousness. You don't have a spirit lurking somewhere in your body, it's not some mysterious floating entity. You are the spiritual being that animates and radiates from the form that you occupy.

However, while the immune system of the body is made up of separate 'helper cells', the immune system of the soul is not separate from the soul/self/spirit. The immune system of the soul is within you, the soul! It cannot be separated from you! I emphasize this in order to underline the understanding that it's distinct from your body! The immune system that is a natural and integral aspect of your being is best described as 'specific movements of consciousness'.

The Three Movements
When the immune system of the soul (self/spirit) springs to life, the three movements within your consciousness are: **awareness, realization and transformation.**

To illustrate how our consciousness moves and works in these ways, imagine you are driving towards a known destination. You also know the general direction in which you want to travel but you're not exactly sure of the route, which has many twists and turns. You've been driving for some time with the **awareness** that you have an uneasy feeling, but you cannot quite put your finger on the cause of that feeling. So you 'stay with' the feeling and deliberately 'look into' the feeling of uneasiness. Suddenly, you notice the sun is shining into the left hand side of the car and you know it should be shining into the right hand side. You **realize** that you are going in the wrong direction. You do an 'about turn' as you 'change' (**transform**) the direction in which you are travelling. The feeling of uneasiness instantly disappears.

Taking the process a little deeper, imagine you become angry towards someone. It seems a normal reaction as it's something you've done, more than occasionally, all your life. Others do it a lot too! But one day, the anger becomes so great you wonder if it's all worth it. You become **aware** of the intense feeling of dis - ease within your self, within your consciousness. You are aware that this dis - ease is the emotion of anger. Instead of waiting to recover, you look into the anger and you **realize** that a) you are its creator and b) the reason you create it is because you 'believe' that others 'should do' what you say (and they are obviously not!). In effect, you implicitly believe that a) you can control others and b) others are responsible for your happiness. You take a moment to consciously challenge those beliefs and you realize they are not 'true'. Of course they are not true - you cannot control others, ever! It may 'appear' that you are controlling them when they do what you say or want, but it's still them deciding to do what they do. It also becomes obvious that others are not responsible for your happiness. However you can also 'see' that it's true to say that while you cannot control others, you can 'influence' others. The **realization** of these 'truths' initiates the **transformation** of your state of being, and consequently your thoughts and behaviors. You cease to attempt to control others. You never become angry towards anyone again and so the dis - ease of angriness is healed! Your energy is now available to focus on the development of creative ways to influence.

You became **aware** of the dis - ease, you looked into it and **realized** the 'causal belief'. You looked a little deeper and realized 'the truth' and, using the power of that truth, you **transformed** your state of being.

Variety of Viruses

While the immune system of the body is designed to identify and heal many types of physical disease, the immune system of the soul (consciousness) is designed to identify and heal many types of dis - ease within consciousness, within 'the self'. Just as any disease in the body is normally due to some invading virus that infects and affects the cellular energy of the body, so all dis - eases of consciousness are also caused by a variety of viruses.

We are now extremely familiar with the idea of 'viruses'. We know how viruses can infect and disrupt the functions of a computer. We now know the many kinds of viruses that can infect and disrupt the functions of our bodies. But what is the virus that infects and disrupts our consciousness i.e. our self? It's called 'belief'. All dis - eases of consciousness are caused by the viruses of different beliefs and our conscious and subconscious 'attachment' to those beliefs. However belief is not the truth. As the old saying goes 'the truth will set you free'. In the context of all the various forms of dis - ease that we create within our consciousness only the realisation of the truth can free us from our attachment to those beliefs and free us from suffering. Hence the three phases of the soul's immune system as it carries out the healing process.

The A.R.T. of Healing

Awareness - Realization - Transformation

Phase 1 - Awareness of the symptoms

This means noticing there is dis - ease occurring within your consciousness i.e. within you! It means being aware of anything from a quiet sense of uneasiness to turbulent thoughts and feelings about anything or anyone.

Being self-aware is not something that comes easily to most of us. We are almost totally programmed to be aware only of what's going on 'out there' in the world around us. We are weather aware, what's on TV aware, what others are doing and wearing aware, news aware, what we are doing tomorrow aware, what's for dinner aware, money aware etc. But the one thing we are seldom aware of is what is going on within our consciousness, within our self. We find it hard to 'notice' the unlimited variety and quality of thoughts and feelings we are constantly creating in our reactions and responses to the world.

We are vaguely aware that our emotions have an effect on our body. But we tend not to notice the presence of the emotion until it has actually reached the physical energy of our form and we 'feel' something physically. Worry affects our stomach, fear affects our heart, tension affects our muscles, anger affects our blood pressure. Consequently we tend to attribute emotions and feelings 'only' to our body and don't realize all our emotions have their origin within our consciousness, within our self.

Another consequence of this unawareness seems to be that most of us don't have a 'developed language' to describe what we feel and the emotions that arise. Without that shared language, it becomes hard to ascribe meaning to whatever is happening within our consciousness, within our self. One of the easiest, and some would say necessary, ways to enhance our self-awareness and develop our language is to talk about what we notice is happening within our consciousness. Not in a formal therapeutic way, but in informal and reflective ways with friends and acquaintances. Priceless is the friend with whom we can be totally open and relaxed as we exchange what we are thinking and feeling about anything and everything. As we do, we co-create a language and we start to see with greater clarity the connections between our beliefs and experiences, between our perceptions and our emotions, between our attitudes and feelings, and between our memories and behaviors.

We don't need to study for a degree in psychology, simply develop a degree of awareness and an ability to describe the what, how and why we think and feel the way we do.

When such interactive conversations are complemented with time spent in quiet self-reflection, occasionally drawing on insights that we find within the wisdom of others, it gradually enhances our awareness and understanding of what's going on within our own consciousness. We start to see clearly how and why we create the many dis - eases of consciousness and how they sabotage the wellness of our being. This is not navel gazing but a self motivated 'inner education' in the only real school in life, which is consciousness itself. It doesn't take long before we are able to identify and free our self from the main dis - eases of the soul that we all 'learn' to suffer from. We explore them all in detail here and, as we do, you will come to see exactly what needs to be 'unlearned'.

Phase 2 - Realization of the Cause

This means 'seeing' through the feelings of dis - ease and realizing the 'viral belief' that has 'infected' our consciousness. This is only possible when we don't avoid the emotions that we feel, and look into and through those emotions. Only then can we 'see' exactly which 'viral belief' sits behind the emotion and is causing the dis - ease. Once again this requires quiet contemplation and perhaps some clues from someone who has already realized the causal beliefs of such dis - eases. Then it's possible to induce the AHA moment which means, "Now I see why I am feeling like this, why I am so upset, why I am feeling so angry, why I am just plain scared. Now I see and realize the underlying belief that I keep empowering that is shaping these thoughts and emotions at the heart of this dis - ease."

As we will discover, all our dis - eases of the soul have symptoms called 'emotion'. All emotion is a form of suffering. That last sentence is difficult for many to accept, usually because they have never seriously thought about or defined 'emotion' itself. To do so requires some time and attention to reflect on our own personal 'insperience' of emotion. Only then can we develop our understanding of the emotions that we are creating and feeling. Only then is it possible to identify and articulate exactly which emotions we are feeling and, in particular, why we are creating those emotions in the first place. This is a gradual process which proceeds according our level of interest!

As we grow up, most of us learn to believe that we have positive and negative emotions such as fear and love, anger and joy, hate and compassion etc. We never really question that belief! But when we notice ALL our emotions have their origin within our consciousness AND when we realize that within consciousness there is no duality, no polarity, no opposites, these 'beliefs' about emotions start to fly out the window. There are no positive or negative emotions. There is just emotion, or not, as the case may be!

At this point many people end their interest in self-awareness and self-realization. You may even be thinking this is getting a bit too deep and too complex, and that life just needs to be lived, not analyzed like this. Besides how can there NOT be positive and negative emotions? But in reality, this is where the healing of all our dis - eases, all our sufferings', all our stress and unhappiness, begins. This is the frontier beyond which you may rediscover the reality of an authentic and sustainable happiness without any dependency on anything or anyone. But it requires seriously challenging and casting aside many of our 'learned beliefs'. Including the belief that there are positive and negative emotions. There are only emotions. Love is not an emotion! It's a state of being. Authentic happiness is not an emotion. It is a state of being. Pure joy is not an emotion, it's a state of being.

Emotion 'happens' when the energy of our consciousness is distorted and it loses its highest vibration, which is it's natural state. That 'highest vibration' is what we call love. But to converse about all of that, we first need to agree on what we mean by 'love', what we mean by 'emotion', what we mean by 'feeling' and what we mean by 'state'. It's not a conversation that many people have, hence the general absence of clarity around the subject of emotion. We'll return to that in a moment.

Realization in this context means seeing and realizing the exact belief within our consciousness that is causing whatever dis - ease (emotion) we are feeling at any given moment.

For example one belief that causes much of the emotional 'dis - ease of fear' is that *life is a survival course*. One belief that causes the 'dis - ease of insecurity' is that *wealth can only be measured by money*! One belief that causes the 'dis - ease of irritation' is that *the table should be laid out exactly the way I like it*!

Realization also means re-awakening to a deeper truth that we already know but has slipped out of our awareness. In those examples, 'the truth' might sound like: *life is not a survival course but an opportunity to be of service to others, real wealth is an inner resource of consciousness known as virtue* and our *happiness is not dependent on the way a table is set*! When we realize such truths, they naturally replace the beliefs and thereby cure the dis - ease. Truth is the catalyst for the third stage of the healing of the soul, which is transformation.

Phase 3 - Transformation of our state of being

Transformation takes place within the self through the rediscovery of what is 'true'. Only the realization of 'the truth' can overpower and replace a 'viral belief' that is always the cause of dis - ease. Healing in this sense means restoring the energy of consciousness to its 'true' state or vibration. That this has happened is confirmed by the disappearance of the feelings of dis - ease. They are replaced by feelings such as peace and contentment, compassion and co-operation, and intentions such as caring and understanding. These are 'emotionless movements' of consciousness which shape attitudes and behaviours that create harmonious connections and healthy relationships with others.

But how do we know that we know or have realized what is true? What is the difference between belief and truth? We used to believe the world was flat. Then we saw a photo and realized the truth, that the world is round. You could call that an 'outsight'! Some people 'believe' that their happiness comes from 'outside in'. You could say this is a 'flat earth' belief! Many others have contemplated their own 'insperience' and realized the truth, that happiness is an 'inside job'. They have had an 'insight' that happiness arises from within our consciousness. We each have the power to create our own levels of happiness from 'inside out'.

Perhaps you still 'believe' other people make you feel angry. But ask the more enlightened around you and they will likely say they have realized 'the truth' that no one ever 'makes' you angry. We each 'create' our own emotions and anger is just a 'popular emotion'! They would say that they have realized that each and every reaction/response is our creation and is therefore our responsibility. They would probably say that it's the realization of that truth, and the restoration of the ability to choose our feelings that comes with it, that has transformed the way they relate to others and live their life.

Most people learn to 'believe' that love is acquired, so they go forth in search of love in life. That seems to be contradicted by those who say they have realized one of deepest truths in life, i.e. love is what we are when we give of our self without condition. So there is no need to search anywhere for love. It's already 'here'! In fact, they remind us that it's a futile search that will only create many moments of dis - ease!

When a truth is realized by the self, it produces a shift in perception which in turn changes our thoughts and actions. Each of these realizations then has the power to change our state of being and the consequent behavior. They have the power to heal the soul, which means eliminate the many kinds of dis - ease that we are habitually creating and feeling within our consciousness.

Both the location and the process of realization and transformation are little understood, even it seems amongst many schools of enlightenment. Imagine squeezing your body into a cardboard box half your height. Your body is in the box but it's lost its 'natural shape/stature'. There will be much physical discomfort. And so it is with our consciousness. There is a natural state of being from which emanates a natural vibration of the spiritual energy that we are. Sometimes we call that vibration peace, at other times we vibrate as love, and sometimes we vibrate as joy or compassion or patience etc. These are natural states of being that we will also 'feel' in such moments.

Mind what you do...in your Mind!

We lose the ability to vibrate from these natural states and extend that vibration into thought and action when we squeeze our 'self' into something unnatural and thereby distort the true nature of our being. We do this by losing our self 'in' what is on our own mind. The boxes are ideas, images, memories and beliefs. We create them in our mind and then squeeze our 'self' into them. We take the shape of what is on our mind. It may be for only a few seconds or a habit of many years! This is sometimes referred to as attachment. Attachment happens when we lose our self in what is on our mind. We don't even realize we are doing it. We then 'identify' with what we are attaching to and that is the moment ego is born. Which is why one of the simplest definitions of ego is 'misidentification'.

When we lose our sense of self in what is on our mind it's as if the conscious being that we are is disformed. We are allowing an idea, image or belief to shape us. We are using the idea/image/belief give our self a false sense of identity. It's as if we cease to be the 'free spirit', that is our true state, and we become 'trapped in' a mental form. Some of the signs we are doing this include feelings of being small, inadequate, threatened, fearful, saddened, stressed, angry, and many other emotions that signal dis - ease! This is why the ego i.e.

misidentitfcation, is the underlying cause of all dis - ease, all suffering. It's not the 'direct' cause of pain, which is physical, but it is the direct cause of all suffering.

Transformation is the liberation of the self from the 'unnatural' forms that the self has created and adopted within the mind. By now I'm sure you have surmised that the self is not the mind. The mind is a function of the self, it is an attribute or faculty of consciousness.

For example, as soon as you start to argue with someone, it means you have become 'the form' of the belief that you are holding in your mind in those moments. You don't notice you are doing this because you are busy either building your defense against the other's belief or your strategy to attack the other's belief. In such moments your belief is shaping you. You are losing your self in the belief that is 'on your mind' and you are therefore perceiving the other's belief as a threat to you. It's personal! But the moment you realize the belief you have created in our mind is just another belief and that it's not you, then you are starting to 'let go'. You are starting to 'come out' of the belief. As you do you are transforming. You are returning your self to your true form as a free spirit, no longer trapped in anything on your mind. That's also the moment the dis - eases of fear and anger, that are the currency of exchange in any argument, start to fade away.

There are three meanings buried in the word 'transformation'. 'Trans' means **TRANSCEND**, 'form' means **FORM** and 'ation' means **ACTION**.

The action of transcending form takes place within consciousness. It is the moment 'the self' stops being shaped by whatever form (image/idea) is on the mind. The self comes out of the mind and thereby rises above (transcends) what is on the mind. The freedom of the self is restored as it returns to its original form as the radiant, invisible, undistorted energy of consciousness. The feeling is one of peace and freedom. The true intention of the self, which is one of 'giving of one's self' without condition, without wanting, is restored. And the actions are felt and seen by others to be kind and benevolent...at ALL times.

The main outward sign of transformation is the absence of emotion and restoration of our capacity to respond creatively instead of react emotionally. Not because emotion is bad or is suppressed or repressed, but it is no longer created! Emotions (energy in motion) are the price we pay today for our attachments (misidentifications) yesterday! In other words, emotions arise within consciousness when the self attaches itself to what is on the mind. If you scream in anger when someone breaks your Ming vase, it means you were attached to and identified with the 'image' of the vase in your mind. If you were not attached to the image of the vase, if you had not lost your sense of self in the image of the vase, you would not create the emotion of anger, you would not suffer from the dis - ease of anger as the vase breaks into a thousand little pieces! You would respond peacefully and forgivingly because it's just a vase and you are you! When you are peaceful and forgiving, you are not emotional, you are at peace and extending love (your self) as forgiveness to the other!

Choosing your Feelings

One of the main signs of 'transformation' is the restoration of your ability to choose your feelings at any and every moment. You may have noticed that this is impossible when you are emotional! When you are emotional, you cannot choose your feelings. This is another clue as to why 'love' is not an emotion. When you are in a loving state you can choose the appropriate way of expressing that love. Perhaps as care or compassion, as acceptance or forgiveness, as kindness or understanding etc. As you extend your self as love in the appropriate way you will 'feel' whatever form you choose to give it. But notice you cannot do that when you're upset, scared or sad. There is just upsetness, which is extremely emotional, there is just fear, which is extremely emotional, or there is just sadness, which is extremely emotional. In such moments, it's as if your ability to choose any other feeling has been switched off.

When we believe and say that love is just another emotion, that's actually what sabotages our ability to extend love to others. When we worry about someone, we believe we are caring, we believe we are being loving. But worry is a form of fear, not love. When we are 'emotional', we are mostly busy with our own emotions, busy with the emotion that 'I am feeling', and therefore not fully available to 'care' for the other. Care is love in action with the intention to benefit the other. But the worrier can't see that as they are busy creating images of what 'might' happen and how 'they' will feel if something does happen to the one whom they are worried about! Phew! It's no wonder the true meaning and feeling of love is so easily lost!

Emotional Intelligence is an Oxymoron!

It's also useful to notice that emotion arises as soon as we 'believe' we are not getting what we want (anger) or when we 'believe' we are about to lose what we 'believe' we already have (fear). Notice that whenever you desire anything you already have whatever it is that you desire as an image or an idea in your mind. You become attached to the image. Then you start becoming busy worrying that it may not show up in the reality of matter, time and space! Love, as we know, has nothing to do with wanting, getting and keeping. Love is definitely absent when we are crying our emotional tears after a perceived loss. This is why 'emotional intelligence' is an oxymoron! When you are emotional you are, in reality, sabotaging your capacity to be intelligent, to make intelligent decisions and offer intelligent advice! More about emotion to come, as it is the main symptom of all the dis - eases that we create and suffer from within our consciousness!

The process of transformation begins when you realise you are attached to a belief that is causing the feeling of dis - ease. But we won't fully let go of the belief which means 'come out of' the belief until we also realise a deeper truth that already exists within us. However, it's hard to see most of the beliefs that we are attached to as they are buried deep within our subconscious. They are part of the 'programming' that we all absorb and assimilate from other people and the world around us as we grow up. This is why it's not enough to be aware of the dis - ease that is occurring within our consciousness. It's not enough to use some kind of 'technique' or receive some kind of therapy to assuage our emotional dis - ease. It's only the symptom. It's necessary to look into and through the emotions that we feel in order to see the causal belief, and then through the belief to realize the truth. It's the realization of truth that empowers us to fully let go of the belief, to detach our self from the belief, to no longer be shaped by the belief!

Detachment does not mean that you don't care or that you are avoiding things, events and people. It means that you are no longer losing your sense of self in what is in your mind at a conscious or subconscious level. It's only in a state of non-attachment that you can 'be your self', that you can be all that you are which is the 'I' that says, "I am"! Only then are you fully free and available to extend the loving warmth of your heart as you genuinely care for others, where before you were just busy with 'me, mine and my emotions'.

Is YOUR Immune System Working?

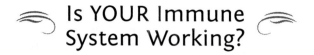

While the immune system of the body can be weakened or impaired by an unhealthy diet, physical exhaustion or viral infection, it is always working to some degree. The immune system of the soul however can be almost completely suppressed. A total absence of self-awareness really means an inability to recognize what is occurring within our consciousness, within our self. When that happens, we are at our most vulnerable to the invasion of the viruses known as 'other's beliefs'. With almost no self awareness we are easily influenced as we start to absorb and assimilate such beliefs as; *it's both natural and necessary to suffer in life; life is just a survival course so be fearful and make sure you look after number one; your success and security will be measured by how much money and stuff you can accumulate.*

Our belief that these beliefs are truths, blinds our awareness to the emotional signals that are telling us that we are 'insperiencing' some dis - ease as a result living by such beliefs. The awakening of the immune system of the soul is essentially the same as the reawakening of self awareness. It starts when we notice and become aware of (conscious of) our emotional discomforts, when we become aware that emotion itself is uncomfortable and realize that it is unnatural. It continues with the 'realization' that we are totally responsible for all our emotions, all our discomforts, all our moments of dis - ease!

Imagine a light bulb in a room. Also in the room is a sensor. Whenever the intensity of light radiating from the bulb goes below a certain level, the sensor will trigger an alarm. Our consciousness is like light, a radiant source of what is often called the light of spirit, or spiritual light. When the frequency, the intensity, the vibration of our consciousness, goes below a certain level, we have an in-built sensor called 'our feelings' that signal to us that something is not OK 'in here'. Unfortunately we have learned to ignore our in-built sensor or even switch it off.

It could also be likened to the security system in a car. You don't understand how the security system works until you get the manual and read the instructions. Most of us don't understand how the sensor system of our consciousness works. No one gave us a manual and no one taught us how to be self aware. We don't know how to register and read our own feelings. We are unable to activate our 'sensor system', recognize the emotions that we feel and to know exactly what is causing those emotions. Our inner sensor system is the gateway to the immune system of the soul as well as its primary function.

It usually takes a certain intensity of suffering for us to start taking notice of our 'feeling sensor'. We will tolerate our dis - eases as long as we can before we start to sit up and notice that we are receiving a signal that is calling us to change something, which means realise something, within our self. When we do eventually start to take notice, there is usually no going back!

PART TWO

The 12 Dis - Eases of the Soul

be·lief
An acceptance without evidence that something exists or is true.
That which is 'thought' to be true but is not 'known' to be true.

truth
That which is true and is verifiable by direct experience. That which never changes.
Synonyms - verity - reality - fact - veracity - fidelity!

As in Body so in Soul

There are a variety of dis - eases of the soul that we have all 'learned' to create and suffer from. Each one has its own causal 'viral belief', its own symptoms in the form of its own thought patterns and its own type of emotional suffering.

The dynamics of many of the dis - eases of the soul are remarkably similar to the diseases that affect the energy of our body. I've used the names and indeed the nature of some of the most common physical diseases as 'metaphors' to describe the dis - eases of the soul.

Some will say there is a direct link between the two, that dis - ease within the soul is the true cause of the diseases of the body. That now seems to be an obvious truth. But that's another seminar! The aim here is to help you to identify the various dis - eases that you have developed within you, the spiritual being, so that you can take your own steps to restore a state of wellness to your self.

As you proceed through each of the 'dis - eases', exploring the causes and symptoms, at the end of each section there are a few questions for your personal reflection. I would recommend you have separate journal in which to scribble your answers to the questions. As you do you start to awaken and fine tune your awareness of what is exactly going on within...you! It's only the ongoing practice of such self reflection, over a period of time, that you break your depence on others insights and wisdom and truly start to cultivate your own.

Everything that you read here points to what you already know. It's only been temporarily lost from your awareness.

1

"I must have more"

The Dis - Ease of ADDICTION

This is not only a disease that affects body and brain. ADDICTION is also a dis - ease of consciousness. The main symptoms to be aware of are DESIRING and CRAVING.

When you look into and behind all desire, you will notice the underlying cause is the 'viral belief' in 'acquisition and possession'. You believe that you can acquire and possess. The arising thoughts include, "I want...," " I need to get...," "I must have...." The body and brain tend to crave 'tangible' things, substances which provide sensual, physical stimulation. The soul's cravings however, can range across many 'intangibles' from knowledge to recognition, from acceptance to affirmation, from status to respect. We all know that when we don't get what we want, we create the emotions of disappointment and frustration, which belong in the families of sadness and anger. These are not moments of happiness, but moments of suffering, moments of dis - ease!

In the context of human consciousness, only the realization of the 'truth' can transform/heal the dis - ease of desiring/craving. Only the reawakened 'truth' can overpower and eliminate the 'viral belief'. Belief is not the truth. Belief is what we create when we lose awareness of what is true, which in the context of our 'being' means the loss of our 'trueness'! In this instance, the truth is restored when you realize that you are consciousness and not form, and that consciousness, i.e. you, needs to acquire nothing!

In TRUTH, I/you/we do not need to acquire anything. Our body 'needs' food, clothes and shelter, but 'I/you/we' do not 'need' to get and keep anything! If there is a need it is to 'take care' of our body, it is to 'give care' to the form we occupy. However, even that is not so much a need as a natural responsibility.

Dependent on Others

Most of us are born, bred and brought up on the belief that we need to acquire the acceptance and approval of others, the affirmation and validation of others. We believe that only then can we feel worthy, feel of value to others and thereby achieve success in life. Many of us will spend our entire life building our reputation in the eyes of others, believing that it's the way to a happy and fulfilling life. A significant number will deeply crave not just acceptance and approval, but the applause of others, as they attempt to build an image in the eyes of the world and make a claim to fame. These are the viral beliefs that sit behind our neediness, our cravings.

When those approvals and affirmations dry up, and our cravings go unsatisfied, we start to feel a lack of worthiness. We consider our self to be inadequate and of no real value. We fear that this failure to acquire and satisfy our desire for others' approval and recognition will continue. So we oscillate between the dis - eases of fear and sadness. Then, whenever we are on the receiving end of the opposite of what we crave i.e. whenever we receive the slightest criticism or the 'hairy eyeball' of authority that conveys disapproval in one glance, we are devastated, eventually angered and then worried that it may happen again.

However as long as we 'believe' we are only a physical form, we will believe our neediness is justified. Our bodies do have needs and if we believe we are just our body, which is what most of us have learned, we then believe that, "I have needs." The realization of the truth that 'I', the being of consciousness, don't need anything will elude us until there is the realization or our 'true identity', which is a spiritual identity, which is not really an identity, more a state of 'true self awareness'.

Until we can free our self from our neediness of others' approval and acceptance, it will be difficult to heal the dis - ease of addiction. It will be hard to end our desiring/craving for the affirmation and validation of others and, for some, the applause of the world. It will be hard to end the emotional suffering that must accompany our neediness.

All because we 'believe' we need to get something from others.

Can you Set your Self Free?

So the question here is can you be OK in your self without being approved of, accepted and applauded by others? Can you live contentedly without needing to know you have a great reputation in the eyes of others? Can you still be calm and cool in the face of any criticism that may come your way? Can you build a relationship free of any kind of psychological neediness within that relationship? If you can say yes to all of the above, then you will be free of one of the most common dis - eases of the soul and suffer no more.

It all hinges on the realization you are not your form, which definitely does have needs. It depends on your realization that YOU are not your BODY IMAGE, as we seem to like to call it today. As long as you believe you are just a body image you will never be content, satisfied or sustainably happy, simply because your body is never as good as that of someone else and it's always in a process of continuous decay! And it seems to have a fixed destination known as it's 'immanent demise'! Not exactly the recipe for a happy life.

At the heart of most wisdom paths and spiritual teachings is a basic truth that can be realized by anyone. You are the formless being of consciousness which animates the form of your physical body. When realised you will notice your 'natural inclination' is not to 'get something from' others and the world, but to 'give something to' whoever is present with you in the moment. If there is a grand design, you might sense that we have all been designed to give of our self i.e. to 'radiate outwards'. It will start to feel unnatural to try to acquire and possess anything from anyone. It will start to seem ludicrous to want those intangible things like the approval and acceptance from others. This one 'realization', the realization of self as the formless being of consciousness, does require some introspection and usually the practice of some method of meditation, until it is firmly restored to our awareness. It is the launch pad into what is often referred to as 'spirituality' or living a more spiritual life.

In summary, the main symptom of the dis - ease of addiction to be **aware** of is the craving for intangibles such as the affirmation and validation of others in order to sustain our self worth and a reputation in the eyes of others. The dis - ease is the feeling of 'fearfulness', that you will be denied these intangibles and that your reputation may be trashed. The 'viral belief' is 'I need to acquire'. The **realization** is that, while your body has needs, we/you/I ultimately need nothing. The truth is we already have all that we need within 'the self', within our consciousness.

However one of the many paradoxes on an athentic spiritual path is you cannot 'know' what is within you until you give it away! **Respect** others unconditionally and you will quickly notice your neediness to be respected diminishing. **Celebrate** others and you will notice how you start to generate a natural appreciation and gratitude for life. The joy of living begins to arise from within your self. This strengthens your resilience when life throws up challenging circumstances. **Care** for others and you will notice how the energy of that caring enhances a feeling of being a source of love for others. This naturally strengthens your awareness of your own value.

One of the main signs that there has been **transformation** and that your addictions are on the wane is when you can remain undisturbed when people don't praise you, don't congratulate you, don't give you approval and may even ignore you. Then you know that the addiction is no more, the 'neediness' habit has been healed. You feel well within your being again.

Personal Reflection

Take a few moments with your personal journal and contemplate the three movements of consciousness that will facilitate your return to wellbeing.

Awareness: Identify the last three occasions when you consciously sought the approval and/or acceptance of another.

Realization: Why do you think you needed to get their approval/acceptance/validation?

Transformation: Imagine you no longer needed their approval/acceptance. How would you feel? What would your attitude feel like and your behavior look like?

2

"That belongs to ME!"

The Dis - Ease of BLINDNESS

There is a Dis - Ease of consciousness that could be called BLINDNESS; not blindness of our physical eyes, but blindness of our inner eye, our third eye, the eye of our awareness. The main symptom is EMOTION. Being emotional is the equivalent of having sand thrown in your physical eyes. However, emotion is a sand we throw in our own eye! Notice, whenever you become emotional, it's as if you can't see (perceive) clearly, can't think clearly or make accurate decisions.

Similar to the dis - ease of addiction, the 'viral belief' that is causing our emotional suffering is 'mineness'! The arising thoughts include, "That's mine..." or "That belongs to me..." or "I own that..." This is our old friend attachment at work again! It seems that few are aware that all emotion arises from the attachments that we create within our consciousness. Only the realization of the truth that no thing and no one is ever mine i.e. is ever possessed by me, can set us free and thereby heal the dis - ease of blindness that is caused by emotion.

Love is Lost...Temporarily!
When we do get what we want at a material level, it's often followed by thoughts like, "I love those things..." or "I'd love

to have one more of those things..." This is another instance when the true meaning of love tends to be lost. In this instance, love is confused with desire and attachment. Love is not desire and it's not attachment. Both are conditional and selfish. This is also where, for most of us, 'love' is mixed up with 'emotion.' Emotion arises out of desire and attachment and is then mistakenly called love. Love and joy are not emotions, they are our most natural states of consciousness when we are non-attached. But we lose our ability to be 'love' and to be 'joy' when we distort the energy of our consciousness with any kind of attachment. Notice, when you become attached to anything or anyone it will eventually, if not immediately, generate fear and sadness; fear of loss or damage, and sadness when inevitable loss occurs. This is why insecurity quickly sets in after the novelty of the attachment ('that is now mine') wears off.

From Dis - ease to Ease

"That's mine and I love it" or "That's going to be mine and I will love having it," are signs we are confusing love with fear. You can recognize this by becoming more aware of what you are feeling. Take a moment and notice for your self the difference between 'feeling fearful' and 'feeling loveful.' When you are fearful notice how you are somewhere in the process of wanting, taking and keeping. You are closed. When you are loveful you are in the process of giving and sharing. You are open. Unfortunately whenever we say, "I love that...," about anything, it usually means, "I am attached to that or to them..", which is the wanting/taking/keeping mode! Fear is dis - ease and love is ease!

Whenever we say, amidst our tears, "I have lost a loved one", what we really mean is, "I have lost an attached one". Sadness is the dis - ease and joyfulness is the ease. But then many will ask how can we be joyful when someone dies? Perhaps by celebrating the time spent together, appreciating the memories they left us and blessing them by sending them our good wishes for the next chapter of their journey! Celebrating, appreciating and blessing are all faces of love in action. When we wear such faces sadness becomes impossible.

But for most of us, this not easy to see, especially when we hold on to the 'viral beliefs' that a) some kind of attachment is OK and b) that ownership/possession is our right. Notice, when you react emotionally to anyone or any situation, the emotion that is arising within your self (from within consciousness) is always because you are attached to something, which can be anything from an idea, an image, a memory or a belief. You are holding onto it and you are trapped in it, within your mind - either consciously or subconsciously, for just a moment, an hour, maybe a year or perhaps a lifetime.

Take a moment at the end of each day, reflect on all such 'emotional moments' until you see what you were attached to. Then you may realize the 'truth about emotion' and how authentic love and joy can only occur when there is no attachment to anything and there is no emotion! Detachment does not mean that you have nothing and no-one in your life. It just means you change your relationship with whatever and whoever is in your life. It means that you fully realize it/they are not 'mine', they are not me! The relationship becomes one of one of non-attachment! Which you ultimately notice is both healthy and empowering, simply because in non-attachment there is no dependency!

Seeing and realizing for our self what is true, within the universe of our consciousness, will include the realization that nothing can ever be possessed or owned. It's as if we intuitively 'know' this truth when we say things like, "Can't take it with you when you go..." or "Here today, gone tomorrow, ah well, that's life." But we fall asleep and lose our natural awareness of this 'truth'. Then the learned, but illusory belief in possession kicks in. It's our belief that attachment is OK and our attempts to make things and people 'mine', that ensures 'emotion' will become the primary currency of exchange of almost all our relationships. Our emotions then become both addictive AND exhausting. It's no wonder we become tired and need frequent breaks and holidays and treatments and therapies and pamperings and ...well, you know the story!

These are the most common forms of attachment and the suffering of blindness that results:

Attachment to an IDEA

As soon as you become attached to an 'idea', perhaps even saying, "This is MY idea," then, whenever someone attacks or criticizes the idea, notice how 'you' become defensive (the dis - ease of fearfulness) and perhaps even attack back (the dis - ease of anger). If you weren't attached to the idea, you'd be more open to others' ideas, you wouldn't lose your peace when the idea that you created was not accepted by others. You would be open to understanding the others' ideas and even learning from them, perhaps looking for creative ways to combine ideas.

Attachment to a BODY IMAGE or any image

If you create an image of your self based on anything in the world, notice how you start to feel insecure (fear). As soon as you create an image of your self in your mind, it's not easy to stay detached from the image. We all learn to create images of our self, usually based on our form as seen on that popular HD channel known as the bathroom mirror each morning! Then if someone laughs at our body or comments negatively about anything to do with the physical image we have of our self, we create 'emotion', usually some form of sadness, anger or shame. In such moments, we are blinded by those emotions. We have lost our peace and are incapable of extending our self as love. All because we are attached to an image we have created of our self within our self. This can only end when we realize, "I am not an image on my mind!"

Attachment to a MEMORY

If someone challenges or tries to correct your memory, notice how you start to defend your interpretation, your detailed description of the event (fearfulness) and even pour scorn on the others' interpretation (anger). Or how you create sadness around the memory, because the moment has gone, it's lost in the past.

Attachment to a BELIEF

Then there is the reason all these moments of the dis - ease of blindness occur in the first place. Which is your attachment to your beliefs - both conscious and subconscious. Which is why it's advisable to not believe anything that you hear or read, but look within your self, and see and know for your self. The way to do that is to build some spiritual practices such as meditation and contemplation into your life.

In all the above examples, we are thinking to ourselves. "My idea, my image, my memory, my beliefs!" It's as if we are attempting to possess and maintain exclusive ownership. This belief in 'mine' is the root cause of all the emotions that momentarily blind us. For some it's not so momentary, more like every day of their lives! It certainly was for me, for a long time.

Emotion is THE most common Dis - Ease of Consciousness

This is a bold statement with which I am sure many would intensely disagree. But before you do too (!), may I recommend you are sure that you know what you 'mean' when you use the word 'emotion'. As it turns out, just about everyone that I encounter in the workshops and in the retreats that I run on this topic, don't have a clear sense of what they mean when they use the word 'emotion'. I am not saying they are wrong, we just don't seem to be able to clearly define emotion, probably because it's just not part of our formal or informal education. "What is emotion?" is not exactly a question teachers ask their class or what families discuss around the dinner table. And that's before we try to pin down the meaning of 'feeling', and then try to untangle the two!

But why is this such a grey area for so many? Three reasons - a) a lack of awareness of exactly what we are feeling at any given moment as no-one really teaches us how to identify our feelings b) an ignorance of the truth that we are 100% responsible for what we feel at all times c) the belief that we are just a body, which then places emotion in the territory of a brain function and consequent body sensation, which we can do very little about. But emotions don't originate in the brain, they originate in consciousness, in the self, in the 'I' that says, "I am." They have an effect on the brain for sure. But we are not the victims of brain function and you can know this the moment you start to notice when, where and how you create your emotions i.e. your sadnesses your angers and your fears!

If we truly realized that we are fully responsible for our emotions and feelings, we would be much more vigilant and quickly learn how to choose and consciously generate our feelings. (There is a complete description of this process in my previous book; The 7 Myths About LOVE...Actually!)

Please don't misinterpret, I am NOT saying emotion is wrong or bad. I am NOT saying we should never be emotional. Emotion is a signal that we are suffering and the cause is always attachment to a belief/image/idea. Emotion is a vital message, a kind of 'inner text' to our self, that we are making some kind of mistake within our consciousness.

Can you see?
See if you can see that dynamic within your consciousness, within your self. Find a quiet corner and reflect on the last time you became upset (emotional). Who created the upsetness? What was the image/idea/belief that you were attached to in your own mind? What was the exact emotion that you created and felt - name it?

As you start to see and name those 'emotions that you feel' within your consciousness, you start to develop the language that makes you 'emotionally literate'. Remember, it's not that emotion is bad or that you should never become emotional. That's not going to happen...overnight! It's beliefs like that which stop us seeing how and why we are creating the emotions in the first place. Only when you 'see for yourself' can you, will you, naturally...stop it!

In essence, the main symptom of the dis - ease of blindness is emotion. When you are emotional, be aware of the exact nature of the dis - ease. Name the emotion and, as you do, you will build your emotional vocabulary and fine tune your awareness. The 'viral belief' that is causing the dis - ease that we all absorb on our way 'up' into our adult life is, "That's mine" or "That will be mine" or "That should be mine." It's the belief that we actually possess...stuff! The realization of the truth is, "Nothing is mine ...ever". The 'truth' is that everything comes and goes, including people, objects, money, thoughts, feelings etc. But there is one thing, which is not a thing, that never comes and goes. It is ever-present. But it's not an 'it', it is not a thing! It is the 'I' that says, "'I am!" And that is what you are - no thing! See that, **realize** that and you are free. You will no longer be possessed by the illusion of having possessions! The **transformation** is seen by the absence of emotion as you no longer cry when anything leaves you, you no longer fear anyone leaving you and you no longer get angry as there is no one to blame when you have nothing to lose! And now you have the ability to welcome and embrace everyone and everything, without holding onto them in any way. Sometimes we call that love! Notice how, when you are in that state of being we call love or 'being loving', there is a total absence of emotion!

Awareness: What are the ten most precious things that you believe belong to you?

Realization: Which of those things do you actually possess, which would you say from your heart is 'mine'?

Transformation: How would you feel 'immediately' after each one is taken away? What would you feel...'eventually'?

3

"I have lost something so precious"

The Dis - Ease of the HEART

There is a dis - ease of our heart; not the heart of our body, but the heart of our consciousness, the heart of our being, our spiritual heart. We know this dis - ease as the specific emotion of SADNESS. We sometimes refer to it as a feeling of heaviness in the heart when we say, "They definitely seemed to have a heavy heart." The 'viral belief' that sits behind this particular emotion and therefore causes all sadness is, "I have lost something/someone." This is one of the most prevalent 'viral beliefs' with which we frequently 'infect' each other, in much the same way that we spread the flu virus around the office! Sadness spreads through our conversations when we 'identify' with anothers apparent loss and generate sorrow on their behalf.

With sadness and sorrow such a common currency in our relationships, they are also 'believed' to be natural. It's hard to realize they are a form of suffering and therefore 'unnatural' events within our consciousness.

Back to Reality!

Returning to the territory of 'what is real' for a moment; in essence there are two realities in life. First is the physical world around us, which is always changing. That includes the physical form that we occupy. The second reality is the world within us, within our consciousness, which is our self. In this reality, while thoughts and feelings change, there is an inner space that never changes. It's the silent and still core of your being. The 'I' that says, "I am," is like the centre of a wheel at which point there is a part of the wheel that never moves. Everything else moves around it. This means that everything 'in life' revolves around the unchanging, unmoving and forever still centre, which is the self. You! Take a moment to reflect and see if you can quieten your thoughts for just... a moment. Allow your self to be aware of nothing but your self being aware. Be aware of the stillness, the silence, that is you! The still, unmoving, unchanging...you.

In between these two realities, between the reality of 'being' (centered) and the reality of 'doing' something in the world (action away from the centre), we have what we call mind. Mind is the interface between being and doing. While your mind is within your consciousness, within 'the self', you are not your mind! The mind is like a window and a screen. Through the window of the mind, you bring the world out there 'in here'...so to speak. At the same time, you can use your mind like a canvas, like a screen, on which to create images, ideas, concepts etc. Through the window of your mind, you then project what you create in your mind 'in here' into the big wide world 'out there'.

Take another moment and see if you can be aware of this process or dynamic.

We all tend to make one fundamental mistake. We 'mistake' the secondary reality of the ever-changing physical world that we bring into our consciousness through our mind, for the primary reality of our self. We learn to 'believe' the only reality is 'out there' in the actions and interactions of all the dramas happening all around us, locally and globally. As a consequence, many of us will never really know, so will never really understand, the primary reality of our own being. As a consequence, we allow the world 'out there' to shape, define and control our state of being 'in here'. Hence the frequent feeling many of us have of being 'at the mercy' of changing events, of being affected by other peoples' behaviors, of being disturbed by others' emotions, of being deeply moved by the movie. We allow the secondary reality 'out there' to overpower us, the self, the primary reality, 'in here'.

The deepest 'viral belief' that keeps us stuck and mistakenly believing that 'the external' is the primary reality is, "I myself am just a physical form." As the old saying goes. "When all you have is a hammer then every problem looks like a nail." When you only believe, see and think about your self as a physical form, then all you tend to perceive, 'value' and want are the material/physical things that you see continuously moving around you. But the moment you awaken and become aware of your self as 'consciousness' itself, the moment you touch and taste that state of still and silent awareness within you, that's the moment you correct your perception of reality and restore awareness of the primary reality, which is the universe of your own consciousness.

Inner and Outer

As you start to become more aware of what is occurring within your consciousness, within your mind, you clearly differentiate between the two realities - the inner and the outer. That's when you start to see the 'connections' between inner and outer, between consciousness and form, between your decisions made in consciousness today and your destiny made in the world tomorrow, between you and your body. In such moments, you are awakening to the primary reality of your being. It's also the moment you begin to heal all these dis - eases of the soul/spirit/self. The viral beliefs behind those dis - eases are seen for what they are, just beliefs absorbed from the secondary reality, from the world itself 'out there'. Against the light of the realized truth that you are spirit not form, those programmed beliefs are perceived for what they are, illusions. They are shimmering illusions passing through you. They lose their power over you as you stop 'believing' and realize what is true. In the case of the heaviness of one's heart, there is the realization that nothing in the secondary reality (the world out there) can ever be possessed by the primary reality (you in here) so nothing can ever be lost. No more loss means no more sorrow!

Look Closely

We live through many frequent moments of sadness in our lives, not realizing we are creating the dis - ease of sadness for our self. When sadness becomes a habit and many moments of sadness accumulate in our memory, depression is not far away. So the **awareness** of the presence of sadness within our consciousness is the first step to healing the dis - ease of a heavy heart. Look into the emotion of sadness that you feel and you will always **realize** the cause is the 'viral belief' that you have just lost some thing/person/reputation/opportunity etc. Keep looking introspectively until you realize that, in reality, you never possessed any of those things in the first place. Allow the realization of that 'truth' to **transform** the heaviness of your sadness into the lightness of being. Watch both your smile and your laughter flood back into, through and out from your consciousness. It will then show up with a smile in the secondary reality of your face!

Let's go one level deeper.

Create another Moment

Sit back, relax and take a moment to watch the world go by. Notice how it's easily getting on with all its moving and changing...without you!

Be still, and notice how you are that stillness at the centre. Just watching ... observing ... being.

Practice that inner state alone and gradually you will start to revive your awareness that the primary reality of life is what is occurring within consciousness, within you, right now.

You will start to notice that all the movements and the changes in everything 'out there' are actually happening within the primary reality of you 'in here', on the screen of your mind.

Now don't go into your mind. Just watch what is happening ON your mind.

The movie called 'Life in the World Out There' is happening on the screen of your mind 'in here'!

It's now playing in the theatre of your consciousness and you are the audience.

Notice, as you just watch, how profoundly quiet and peaceful you feel.

Notice the absence of all emotion, but the presence of a quiet joy, a deep appreciation and gratitude that naturally embraces whatever is happening out there 'in here'!

Be aware of how everyone and everything are just passing through. Not via the airport but via your consciousness as they pass through YOU!

Notice how you are aware that you never pass, you are always...there!

Not even there but...here!

See if you can be aware, that what you previously believed was 'out there' is, in reality, now here!

Sit... relax... watch... see... realize... know.... be.

Reflections for your Journal

Awareness: How would you help another to be aware that to be sad and sorrowful is unnatural?

Realization: What truth would you want to help the other to realize that would help them not to create and feel sorrow after they believe they have lost something precious?

Transformation: How can you demonstrate to others that they can choose not to suffer when they believe something or someone is lost?

4

"Something terrible is about to happen"

The Dis - Ease of PARALYSIS

There is a dis - ease of consciousness that we know as PARALYSIS. The primary symptom is FEAR. It is the emotion of fear that paralyses our consciousness like the proverbial rabbit caught in the headlights. It comes in many shades, from anxiety to panic, from tension to worry, from insecurity to abject terror! We tend not to take much notice of its presence as it's a long-time companion in most of our lives. We learn to live with it, until it dominates our life and may even lead to some form of physical sickness.

It also stimulates a certain addictive chemical in our body called adrenaline. So unaware are we that we will go to a horror movie and pay someone to frighten the living daylights out of our self, in the name of relaxation! Fear, like adrenaline, is addictive. Perversely, that means stress is addictive. So it's no wonder when people are shown ways to become stress-free, they often say something like, "Well stress is a natural part of my life, so I think it must be OK. Everyone has stress so it must be human nature." Which is code for, "I really don't want to change, I am addicted to my stress!"

Notice how sadness is always based on the 'belief' that something in the past has been lost, and fear is always a 'belief' of loss to come, that is projected into an imagined future.

All forms of fear stem from the same 'viral belief' which is, "I am about to lose something." That 'something' could be anything from tangible objects to a personal reputation, from an opportunity to someone's approval, from another person to a position at work. We also 'fear' on another's behalf. We imagine they are going to lose something so we become frightened for them. We might even suffer more than them. Yet, as we explored earlier, so many of us have grown up with that 'viral belief' that says worrying for others is a way of showing we care!

It's easy to say and I have been encouraging you to realize what some call an 'eternal truth' that sounds like this, "I have nothing to lose because ultimately nothing is mine." But it's hard to live after a lifetime of assimilating and affirming the 'viral belief', "I have everything to lose because everything I have is mine."

False Sense of Security

Perhaps we need to ask why would we want to possess or own anything in the first place? It's usually because whatever we believe we possess 'seems' to provide a sense of stability, security and status. It seems to offer a sense of some control in a world that is constantly changing. In effect, we are externalizing our sense of stability and security, and investing them in a changing and unstable world over which we have no control. So asleep are we that most of us don't notice that to make our stability, security and sense of self dependent upon anything or anyone outside our self is to create feelings of...instability and insecurity!

Imagine you own or possess nothing and no-one! Yes, there is the house, the car, the job, the clothes, the wardrobe, the pictures, the partners and maybe even the children. Could it be possible to realize 'they' are NOT mine? They don't actually belong to me! They all come into our life for a reason. Some to teach us something, some to give us the opportunity to give of our self, some simply for functional use, some for convenience, some so that we can co-create with other people. But none are ultimately 'mine'. If you can stand back from them ALL, for a moment, you may get a glimpse of a basic truth that reminds you that all things 'out there' are just 'packets of energy' going in and out of existence as energy is constantly changing its many forms! It's the nature of all energy in the material reality out there to constantly change its form, location and relationship to all other forms.

Companion or Controller?

Even our children are not 'MY children'. They are human beings on their own unique journey through life. We have the privilege and honor to be able to help them on their way; to be a guide, a coach, perhaps a companion, sometimes a counselor, sometimes a teacher, and sometimes to just be a friend. They give us the opportunity to play all those roles and, as we do, we learn, grow and become wiser. In the process, they give us the chance to show, give and get to know what we ourselves have within us. Unfortunately, many parents can't see this. They tend to see only one role, which is 'supreme controller'! Why? Because of one 'viral belief'! I have to control what I believe is mine, MY children. Then we use another 'viral belief' to justify our attempt to control when we say, "But it's for their own good!" Suddenly the parent becomes a part time tyrant and therefore a teacher of the practices and procedures of tyranny!

Can you Lose your Life?

The only way free from fear of loss is the same as the way free from the heavy heart of sadness. It's to realize there is absolutely nothing to lose because nothing is ever ours/yours/ mine! Then some say, "But what if I lose my life? Surely that is one thing that I can lose." Herein lies perhaps the deepest truth which, when realized, will allow you to walk fearlessly everywhere and forever. It sounds like this; *life is what you are. You occupy and animate your body thereby bringing it to life. Your body eventually has to go, that's for sure, but that's not the same as losing your life because you are life and you can never lose your self!* Now there's a meditation on its own!

The End of the Story

The 'story' of the life that you are creating through your body i.e. your life story, may come to an end. But that's just a story 'in life', it's not life itself. They are simply memories you gather and string together along the way, and 'you' are not a string of memories! You are life itself and you can never lose your self. Have you ever lost your self? The self is the one thing that never goes anywhere!

Now, some will even say there is no self. OK let's go down that road for a moment. Who is the one referring to the self as self. There is someone there, yes? OK let's not call it self, let's just call it awareness or the one who is aware of being aware. That's me/you or just 'I'. That is life. That spark of pure awareness is sometimes called soul or spirit or just consciousness. But whatever word we use, the word itself is not it! The word is not me! The word is always inadequate. Just be aware that you are aware, be aware that you are 'liveliness' itself, you are life...itself! Can you grasp your self? No. Can 'you' grasp and hold on to life like the hand of your body can grasp and hold an object, or your mind can hold an idea? No! So if 'you' cannot grasp 'life' you cannot lose life!

When we talk of losing our life, what we really mean are the conditions of our life including our lifestyle, which is what we have created, what we 'know' and have become attached to. Yes, our story about our life and all its material conditions will come to an end. And because we are attached to the memories that make up what we call 'my story' and because we are attached to all the images of all the things and people within 'my story', we identify our self with 'my story'. Stories and the different components within stories have endings, so fear arises. But you have no idea whether 'you', the creator of the story, will end!

Let's say there IS an end of you. What happens in 'the end' is a complete unknown. And you cannot be fearful of what you don't know. It's both irrational and illogical. That's why all fear is based on losing what you believe you already know or have. But what you have are just memories and you are not a memory! You are ...you!

Dying to Live

To be attached to anything or anyone, to any story, including our own or others' stories, is to not live fully. In fact it's a way of suppressing our life energy, our self. As we saw earlier, when we become attached to anything, we become trapped in the idea or image of the thing in our own mind. We become small and limited as we define our self by those small and limited ideas and images that come out of our memory. Next to YOU, even big ideas are small! As a consequence of attachment, the dis - eases of sadness and fear must visit. In order to live and be fully alive, we need to be totally free, so it is necessary to kill our attachments every day. Not literally of course; kill means break the attachment, release our attachment or be non-attached, sometimes described as 'letting go'. But because we were taking our sense of life and living from our attachments, from our story, it feels like we are killing our self whenever we think about 'letting go' of...anything!

The Root Cause of Dis - ease and then Disease

This means that every time we attach to, and identify with, what we are not, we are committing a kind of spiritual suicide. The source of the dis - ease of consciousness that we call stress is always attachment and misidentification. This is the cause of all our fears and angers and we now know it's these emotions that, over time, also have such a detrimental impact upon the health of our bodies. When we create dis - ease and sabotage the wellness of our being, we not only create our own unhappiness, it then affects our physical health by triggering disease in our bodies. This is the 'psychosomatic effect'. So the root causes of both our dis - eases of soul and our diseases of body, is our attachment to the 'viral beliefs' that a) loss is possible and b) possession is possible. These 'viral beliefs' are seldom diagnosed on the journey back to good health and wellness of being.

Living is Dying and Dying is Living!

The bodies that we occupy are our dwellings. Our body is our Rolls Royce! They are exquisite and efficient creations which allow us to create our life and to connect and co-create with others. They are a medium which gives us the opportunity to express, to 'press outwards', the attributes and the beauty of our being. To care for our body is to have the right relationship with our body.

You could also say for your body, that as it lives it is dying. We are all animators of a material form that is in a constant process of physical decay. It's called aging with a destiny called death! So if you are attached to, and identified with, the body you occupy then you will 'believe' that 'I am aging' and that 'I will die'. Hence it's easy to spend your entire life in some state of anxiety! But is it true? Do you die? The scientific jury is out because it's impossible for science to prove that the 'self', as a conscious entity, as a spiritual energy, exists separate from the body. There is much anecdotal evidence in the form of 'out of body' or 'near death' experiences. There are many people who believe they have experienced past lives. There are those who have been hypnotically regressed into recalling past lives. And there are millions who 'intuitively sense' that this is not their first four limbed 'vehicle' and that death is just a gateway to another life, a timely transition into a new model! Each of us can only decide for our self.

The Deepest Freedom
What seems to help that decision, especially if we are in the unsure camp, is the learning and practice of meditation and contemplation. This allows you to see and know, to sense and realize, your SELF, without all the stories, without all the attachments and dependencies, without the baggage of all the inherited beliefs. It allows you to touch and sense a deeper level within your self, within your consciousness. A level where you are attached to nothing and no one. Where you have no memories and where you know the deepest freedom and the greatest joy. You can't 'imagine' it, you can only touch it, be in it and then know it. Only then might the idea of dying lose its finality and perhaps even its actuality!

The Highest State
It's only when you get to the top of a mountain that you get to see the whole of the landscape below in one clear image. It's as if you see the big picture and you feel as if you are the master of all before you. Similarly, it's only when you touch and know that deepest, or should that be highest, state of consciousness where you are attached to nothing, dependent on no-one, without any kind of neediness, a truly free spirit, that you see clearly how all the attachments at those lower levels of consciousness are the causes of all your

fears, all your moments of inner paralysis. Once you have had that taste, it not only gives you a new insight into your self, it also restores your inner power to be unaffected by the comings and goings of all those things you previously held onto for dear life. Instead of feeling powerless to deal with adverse events and circumstances, instead of feeling disempowered by the idea of an inevitable fate, you stand in your power once again.

In summary, be **aware** of any form of fear arising in your consciousness, in you. Look into it and see if you can see the 'viral belief' behind it. You will notice that you believe you are about to lose something or someone in the near or distant future. You will notice that you are misusing your imagination, as you create a movie on the screen of your mind where you are catastrophizing and thereby terrorizing your self. Be quiet as you watch, and see if you can see behind the images and the feelings of your imagined future catastrophic loss. See if you can see a deeper truth, that you do not possess what you believe you may lose! They are just props in one of a million scenes in the story of your life. It's not yours to have. You cannot lose anything that you do not have. 'In reality', you have nothing. When you **realize** this, then the 'false sense of self', that was the result of identifying with what you thought was 'mine', is dead. The false 'you', perhaps many false versions of you, that were sucking your life energy, just died. But YOU are now fully alive. And when there are no more false selves to sustain, then, and only then, can you start to live fully and fearlessly.

For most of us, life is lived through many forms of fear, including anxiety, tension, worry and moments of sheer panic. Letting the 'false selves' die so that you can start to live is liberation from all those fears. Your **transformation** is 'known and felt' only by your self, but it is witnessed and felt by others as they receive a very different quality of energy from you. You feel an internal and highly exhilarating freedom and they see and feel the presence of a free spirit rising.

Your Journal Reflections

Awareness: Write down all the things you believe you will lose in the future. How will you feel when they go? How long will it take to recover from those feelings? (make a list and estimate each one)

Realization: How could you ensure that, when the time comes to be parted from all that is in your life, you will not suffer?

Transformation: How would you feel and what would you do differently if you realized that, in reality, you cannot lose anything?

5

"They should do what I want"

The Dis - Ease of INSANITY

There is a dis - ease of consciousness that we know as INSANITY; not the kind of insanity as defined by the psychiatric universe that would have us 'sectioned'. It's the 'every day' kind of insanity. A popular insanity! The primary symptom is ANGER in one of its many forms. This is the emotional fire that steams up our vision and sends our thoughts in a crazed dash through our mind as we seek justice or revenge. Essentially, anger arises out of the 'viral belief' that we can change or control the two things in life which can never be changed and over which we have no control, namely the past and other people. The arising thoughts sound like, "I am not getting what I want...they are not doing what I want...they should do what I want...I should be more in control of them."

Why insanity? Three reasons. Whenever anger arises, it means we ourselves are out of control as we surrender control of our consciousness to the incendiary emotional disturbance of the anger. Secondly, we become irrational. For some moments at least, we lose all ability to think and decide rationally. Thirdly, and the main reason we can call anger insane, it's a sign that we are trying to do the impossible i.e. change what we can never changed, the past or other people. It's just that we are totally unaware that this is what we are trying to do. Fortunately the anger always passes, as does all emotion, and we eventually calm down. Unless we break the habit of creating anger the emotional fire will simply grow hotter and more frequent.

Celebrating our Unhappiness

Most of us are aware that we are extremely unhappy whenever we are upset. But society approves of our upsetness. Perversely, we even learn to celebrate such moments of unhappy upsetness! So we believe it's OK. Mom and dad didn't disapprove when we threw a hissy fit, as long as it was over quickly! We have all learned to be 'entertained' by the rage and revenge of others, whether in a movie or in real life. Unless of course it's happening to us! So we don't challenge the belief that a bit of anger is OK'!

There are seven popular 'viral beliefs' around anger and its various 'forms' (irritation, frustration, resentment, rage etc.) that infect our consciousness. These beliefs usually ensure we become frequently insane while being completely unaware that we are temporarily off our rocker!

The Viral Beliefs

1   It's natural to be angry, so it's OK.

2   My/our anger might change things for the better 'around here'.

3   It's not healthy to keep your anger all bottled up, so it's good to let it out.

4   It's better to express it, otherwise how will others know what you feel.

5   It's 'them' that's making me angry.

6   I 'need' to get angry from time to time as it motivates me to act.

7   Anger is a way to get things done, it's a way of motivating others (says the lazy parent/manager).

Emotional Pandemic

Are these beliefs actually true? Until truth is realized, our insanity will increase as we continue to create the 'red mist' emotion along a spectrum from a smoldering grumpiness to a volcanic rage!

These beliefs are global and that's why anger, in all its forms, can be classed as an 'emotional pandemic'. Each day brings news of further outbreaks, and the deaths of hundreds and sometimes thousands of people at hands of anger in action. A screaming mob protesting against their government or against another government is a sure sign the virus has been activated, many have been infected and insanity reigns en mass.

Freeing your self from these self-created volcanic eruptions means not only realizing the truth, but living it. Old habits die hard so old ways of reacting angrily are habits that don't disappear overnight. It's useful not to expect instant success. Each day brings many opportunities to wake up, dispel those 'viral beliefs' and live some of the most powerful truths in our relationships at home and at work. In the context of healing the dis - ease known as the 'insanity of the soul', here are some of those truths that, when realized and translated into behavior, will serve to restore the coolness of wellness to an agitated self.

From Belief to Truth

1   **Viral Belief:** It's natural to be angry, so it's OK. **Truth:** No it's not 'natural'. Anger is a sign you have temporarily

lost awareness of, and connection to, your 'true nature' which is peaceful and loving.

2. **Viral Belief:** My/our anger might change things for the better 'around here'. **Truth:** 'Around here' starts within your own consciousness. Anger is a detrimental change in consciousness. Feel it for your self! The physical equivalent is sticking a knife in your leg!

3. **Viral Belief:** It's not healthy to keep your emotions bottled up, so it's good to let it out. **Truth:** It's not a good idea to express angrily as it is a form of violence and violence is the underlying emotional condition of all conflict and war.

4. **Viral Belief:** It's better to express it, otherwise how will others know what you feel. **Truth:** If you keep telling people how angry you are, they are likely to start behaving towards you in certain ways, so as not to 'set off' your angriness. So you are encouraging people to fear you and that fear will eventually turn into 'avoid you' or the thought, "What can I do to set off his anger?" as they try to have power over you.

5. **Viral Belief:** It's 'them' that's making me angry. **Truth:** No-one else ever makes you angry. We are each 100% responsible for our emotional state. (see previous book Don't Get MAD Get Wise)

6. **Viral Belief:** I 'need' to get angry from time to time as it motivates me to act. **Truth:** Anger is not a need, it's a loss of awareness leading to a loss of self-control. If there is a need, it is to stay calm. Only then can you connect with and understand the needs of the other. Only then can you respond proactively instead of reactively. If you use anger to motivate your self, it results in a) emotional dependency/addiction b) the tendency to start consciously looking for reasons to be offended c) continuous unhappiness.

7   **Viral Belief:** Anger is a way to get things done, it's a way of motivating others (so says the lazy parent/manager). **Truth:** Yes, the lazy way to parenting and managing is to use anger to invoke fear in others. You may get what you want done, but you just sabotaged your own happiness and the harmony of the relationship. Time and energy spent repairing both will be necessary.

Sanity starts to return when you become **aware** that the dis - ease of these moments of insanity is increasingly killing your 'joie de vivre'. You also notice that they are sabotaging your relationships, as people around you arrive with the walls already erected in defense against your irritations, frustrations and angriness. But liberation from this dis - ease arrives the moment you **realize** that people and events are not designed to dance to your tune. They are not here to make you happy or unhappy. That's your job.

When you fully **realize** you only have dominion over your own inner world, within your own consciousness, within you, only then will you have freed your self from attempting to control the uncontrollable. You will have restored the inner power to generate your happiness, your joyfulness, your lightness, from the inside. Happiness is, after all, an 'inside job'! Your **transformation** will be complete when no-one, no event and no circumstance, locally or globally, can ever 'trigger' you to create anger ever again. You will be seen skipping and dancing your way through life, metaphorically speaking, refreshed by the realization of one significant truth; to be happy, to know love, and to be at peace are all states of being that you can create at any moment without any help from others or from the world.

Questions for your journal reflections

Awareness: When were the last three occasions you suffered from the dis - ease of temporary insanity know as anger?

Realization: What specifically were you trying to change that was impossible to change that lead to you creating irritation, frustration or full blown anger in each of those situations?

Transformation: Imagine being in the same situations again and not reacting angrily but responding in a cool and rational way - what have you realized that has allowed you to behave differently in those specific situations?

6

"I don't deserve such kindness"

The Dis - Ease of DIABETES

Yes there is a dis - ease we could call 'diabetes of the soul'. At least in this little book there is! At some time in our lives, someone has said or done something inexplicably kind and generous towards us. In such moments, we may have said, "How sweet of you, thank you so much." In that moment, we ourselves have changed the vibration of our consciousness into our own version of a moment of profound gratitude, laced with a gracious sweetness in return. Though we may not have noticed it at the time, that 'sweet vibration' that we created within our self towards 'them' also energized our whole being. In such a moment, we ourselves became softer, kinder, sweeter towards, well... everyone! For a few moments at least!

We may even have noticed that, because we were sweetness and light in return for the sweetness of another, it brought with it the feeling that we may have even more of our own kindness to give. Perhaps the thought arose, "Now why can't I feel like this more often?"

As we are now aware, the physical ailment that we know as diabetes happens when our body loses the ability to produce the chemical which breaks down the foods we eat, which are largely sugars, and then transfer the energy of those sugars into the cells of our bodies, thereby giving fresh energy to our body.

Almost exactly the same happens at a spiritual level, within consciousness, when we suffer from the soul's version of the dis - ease of diabetes. The main symptoms include a shrinking feeling, sometimes a kind of resentful closedness or perhaps a perceptual cynicism towards the presence of another's kindness or sweetness. This signals our inability to be open and accepting of the kindness, the generosity, the sweetness of the other. It's as if we can't accept it, break it down and absorb the energy that comes with the recognition that 'they are being kind to me'. That is what then sabotages our ability to generate the 'reciprocal sweetness' in the form of gratitude in return. It's our reciprocal act that gives us energy, not their gesture of kindness or sweetness. We may use their gesture to feed our ego, but it's our ability to return the gesture, to generate and reciprocate with a simlar energy, that gives us a shot in the spiritual arm!

The breakdown of our capacity to reciprocate tends to happen when we start to consider our self either consciously or subconsciously as undeserving or unworthy of another's kindness or another's love. Something gets in the way and it's usually one of two 'viral beliefs' which sound like, "I don't deserve their generosity and their appreciation" or "They are obviously being nice because they want something from me." Which is code for, "I don't deserve such loving energy, I am unworthy of another's love." In other words, we have created and are carrying either a 'dark and/or distorted self image' or we have developed a habit of being 'cynically suspicious' of others' intentions. This is what kills our ability to assimilate and then reciprocate their kindness, their generosity of spirit, their sweetness, their love.

Spiritual Exhaustion

The extreme spiritual diabetic cannot accept the love of others which also means they cannot give of themselves lovingly. Acceptance is, after all, one of the first ways we express our love. That means they are temporarily unable to generate the sweetness that true love is, within their own consciousness. It's as if the self has lost it's capability to be in it's highest state which is love itself. The energy or vibration of love is then unavailable. The result, similar to the exhaustion of the physical diabetic, is an inner hopelessness, a growing helplessness and certainly an absence of any real enthusiasm for life in general or to be with others in particular. When we lose our ability to be in a loving state we find it hard, and sometimes impossible, to 'give' in return for the loving energy of another. As a result a spiritual exhaustion eventually sets in.

It doesn't help to start trying to 'love your self'. Many believe this will remedy a feeling of the lack of love in their life. But it won't work because it's impossible to love one's self. To say or even just think, "I love my self," implies a subject and an object, and there are not two selves. That's why 'trying' to love one's self causes another kind of dis - ease called 'fragmentation'! Love is only 'known' to the self when the self has the intention to give, to extend towards and connect with others or with the natural world. Love is the energy of the soul, the self, when given selflessly i.e. with no thought of acquiring anything for the self. To try to love oneself is not only impossible but it has a selfish motive! Thinking, "I need to love my self," is really code for. "I need to get love for me from my self." Which is almost, just, well...a bit daft! There is no 'I' that is separate from the 'self'. But it won't do any harm to keep 'trying', at least our attention is on love and being loving!

Waves and Oceans

Love is just a word we use to describe the highest vibration of the energy of the self. That's not to say we don't receive and feel love from others. But it's the difference between the wave and the ocean. We will receive waves of loving energy from another. But they pass, as they must, as all waves do! The wave is nothing in comparison to an ocean, to an unlimited source. There is an unlimited source of love within all our hearts. Not the heart of our body, the heart of our soul! You are your heart, you are the soul. The words may seem to differentiate but ultimately all these words i.e. soul, heart, self, consciousness, point at the same 'I' that says, "I am." That unlimited inner source could be likened to an ocean. Waves come and go, but the ocean of this loving potential is always only one second and no distance away within your self. You are it! But you can only be aware of being 'it', you can only be aware of being a source of love, when there is an end to 'wanting' waves of love from others.

The key to drawing on our inner source, our ocean if you like, is intention. Only the accurate intention behind our words and actions allows us to draw on our own inner ocean. As we do, as we give without condition, we may even feel 'oceanic', which is the feeling that we have an unlimited supply of energy to give. When we feel this unlimited source flowing from within us, it brings with it a happiness that we sometimes call bliss. Hence the simplest definition of life in six words: peace is...love does...happiness rewards!

Receiving is Giving

But that's not so easy in a world where we learn to believe that we need to find love, get love, win love, be loved, before we can know love. All these ideas are 'viral beliefs' that will ultimately cause the 'diabetes of the soul', which is the inability to convert the loving gestures of others into the sweetness that will energise us to be capable of reciprocating with the sweetness of our own love.

To accept the love of another is an act of love in itself because you are 'giving' them the opportunity, the porthole, through which they can pour their love. That's when they realize their own sweetness. Only in a truly loving state is receiving an act of giving. But we tend to sabotage that state with the 'viral belief' that we cannot, should not, must not wait to receive, we must go and get it! In short, we 'want'.

So there, in a nutshell, is why the vast majority of people on planet earth today suffer from the dis - ease known as 'diabetes of the soul' - some people some of the time and some people almost all of the time and probably most of us most of the time!

From Head to Heart
Special diets and certain drugs help the diabetic to manage the physical condition of diabetes. High quality company and the detoxing of our consciousness from all the 'intangible drugs' (See Dis - ease No 1) that are our dependencies can help the soul with what we could call 'spiritual diabetes'.

Being in unconditionally loving company, the 'spiritual diabetic' slowly relearns how to accept the love of others, which is the same as learning how to be love themselves. This helps them move towards that moment when they are able to restore their ability to reciprocate from the heart and not the head. In other words, to give love, to be loving and 'mean it'.

However the drugs that we use as a substitute for love will need to go. Those substitutes are our dependencies. Whatever we have become dependent on for how and what we feel is a drug we are using to assuage our temporary inability to be loving and loveful. Take a moment and write down all the things you are dependent on both physically and mentally, and you will start to see what your 'substitutes' are. What do you currently believe you could not live without? Then imagine living without each of those dependencies and as you do you are rehearsing your freedom, you are preparing your self for a return to your natural loving state of being. You are preparing for the moment when you are free and open and transparent and available and giving...again! Without desiring, wanting, expecting, craving or attracting anything in return!

A cure for the spiritual dis - ease of diabetes is almost complete when you fully **realize** that love is ultimately what you are when the 'energy of you' is radiating outwards at its highest level. It is what we are here to do. Love is what the 'I' that says, "I am" is, in its highest state of being. When that is realized then 'the search' for love is called off. The heart is healed and **transformation** is almost complete.

You may even realize, that when you are authentically loveful towards others, you are fulfilling the very purpose of life itself. In such moments, the energy of the soul, the self, is fully revitalized and exhaustion, helplessness, hopelessness and apathy all become fading memories and extremely strange concepts!

Ultimately you cannot 'manufacture' an authentically loving gesture. It is only 'real' when it is spontaneous and natural. But between here and there it does no harm to do a bit of manufacturing! If nothing else it awakens us to a deeper level of self awareness as we explore and understand the ways in which we block our own heart.

Awareness: From which two people, in your life today, do you find it particularly difficult to receive love in whatever form e.g. sweetness, kindness, care etc.?

Realization: Why do you think you are unable to receive and reciprocate their love?

Transformation: Visualize your self intending and actually giving to each one some form of kindness, completely free of desire for anything in return? (if, at this point, a question arises in your head that sounds like, "What's the point?" it means you have missed the point!) Then create an opportunity to put your vision into action.

7

"I've done something wrong, so I am bad"

The Dis - Ease of Being CRIPPLED

There is a dis - ease within consciousness that makes us feel as if we are mentally and feelingly CRIPPLED. The primary symptom is GUILT. The recurring 'viral belief', which can stay with us for our entire life is, "I have done something wrong, therefore I am a bad person."

Whenever you become aware of feeling guilty, look straight into what you are feeling and you will notice a matrix of emotions. Guilt is a mix of sadness, anger and fear. Three in one! The arising thoughts, that many of us know so well, include, "I messed up again." "They'll never forgive me for this." "How could I have done something so badly." While we can still speak and interact, it's as if we are stunted, stuck, momentarily crippled. It's hard to look the other in the eye. Our head is bowed as we look down and away. We feel drained of all enthusiasm.

In such moments, we certainly don't feel drawn to understand where our guilt is really coming from or how and why we are its creator. However, the realization of the truth about guilt is one of the most freeing and healing processes. But it's deep.

It's About Conscience

It is generally recognized that every human being, regardless of their situation or background, has a conscience as their inner guide. It's just that some seem more able to listen to it and be guided by it than others. Conscience is that in-built capacity that allows us to sense, feel and know the accurate thing to do and the inaccurate thing to avoid doing. I use the terms accurate/inaccurate while deliberately avoiding the terms 'right and wrong' and you'll see why in a moment.

Conscience turns up in almost all religious philosophies, wisdom paths and spiritual teachings. It is generally recognized to be that aspect of our 'consciousness' that is our source of goodness, our virtuous intentions, our inner rudder. It keeps us on the straight and accurate path, known as 'being true to your self' or, more accurately, 'being your true self'. Not truth in an objective, prescriptive and absolutist sense. But 'truth' in a subjective sense, where we are living our life moment-by-moment from an accurate awareness of ourself as spirit not form. When guided by our conscience, we are aligned with our truth, which really means our 'true nature', our 'trueness'. We are open, transparent and loving, attached to nothing and no-one, and therefore our decision-making is free from being skewed by sadness, fear or anger. However, we now don't know our self as we have learned to identify with what we are not, so our true nature, i.e. our 'trueness', has been compromised. Attachment and misidentification creates the noise of emotion and consequently our conscience is harder to hear and to follow.

The Origins of Guilt

While we use the word 'conscience' in different ways, it's most common use tends to be in reference to right and wrong. When we listen to and are guided by our conscience, we are said to be doing the 'right thing'. While the 'wrong thing' is seen as an action or decision against our conscience. We often refer to someone who lives their life with great honesty and integrity as a person of 'good conscience'. We have all heard of the 'conscientious objector'; a person who refuses to blindly follow others into war or violence. They would say that war is an act against the 'true' nature of humanity.

The most common use is when we talk of having a 'guilty conscience'. We all know that moment of guilt when our conscience 'bites' and we think to our self, "I have not done the right thing." But 'in truth', the conscience can never be guilty and it certainly doesn't generate the feeling of guilt. It's the ego that does that. It's the ego that entertains and encourages the judgments of right and wrong. It's the ego that hijacks our conscience almost every day of our life, sustaining the illusions of right and wrong, good and bad. Here is why.

Guilt Gets an Early Start

When we were young and innocent, we 'learned' to become dependent on the approval of others for how we saw our self and felt about our self. The main source of approval was usually authority figures like parents and teachers. When we did something 'right' in their eyes we were given the accolade of 'being good'. At the same time, we found our self receiving a wave of warm 'approving' energy that we mistook for love! But then, only moments later, when we did something 'wrong' in their eyes, we were labelled 'bad'. We were then denied that wave of warm energy to which we had become slightly dependent! It is during these formative childhood moments that we learned to 'believe' in other people's ideas of 'right and wrong' and to immediately and personally associate them with, "I am good" or "I am bad." We learned that we were sometimes a 'bad person' and at other times a 'good person', but that we should always try to be a good person. And so, when it was deemed we had done something wrong and therefore bad, we were encouraged to create the feelings of guilt as a kind of punishment and therefore a corrective measure. Not least because it allowed those big people to sustain their illusion that they had us and our emotional state under their control!

The Emotions of Guilt

The dynamic by which we create guilt is revealing. If you did take that moment to look into guilt from your own experience, you will have noticed the matrix of those three emotions – sadness, anger and fear. Like all emotions, they are not created by others but by our self. As we saw earlier, sadness always follows a sense of loss. Anger is the projection of our suffering, in the form of blame. And fear is either fear of the future recurrence of such loss or fear of being found out (future loss of reputation/approval).

So let's correlate this emotional matrix with the ideas of good and bad/right and wrong. As children, we learned to 'oscillate' between the self images of 'good person' and 'bad person', depending on the judgments of those 'big people', whom we innocently believed at the time. When they told us we were good, we believed them and created an idea/image in our mind of our self being good. Similarly when they said to us we were bad, we created a subtle image within our minds of being a bad person. So when someone judges us negatively, including our selves judging our self negatively, we have the tendency to re-energize the 'I am a bad person' self-image. It's as if the 'I am a good person' self-image, which is obviously preferred because it came with a wave of what we thought was love, is then 'lost', hence the 'sadness component' of guilt.

In life in general, anger is most often directed at others, but the 'anger component' in guilt in particular is usually directed towards our self for what we perceive is a self-inflicted loss of the self-image 'I am a good person'. The 'fear component' of guilt is most often based on the possibility that others will find out that we have 'done bad' and we will therefore lose our reputation in the eyes of others or lose the approval of others!

This is all ego's game simply because all ego is based on a 'mistaken self identity'. In the case of guilt, our self-identity is based on an image of 'being good' and, when we seem to contradict that image with 'bad behavior' or even bad thoughts, we create feelings of guilt, a combination of the emotions of sadness/anger/fear within our self.

To feel guilty is to feel disempowered and to show that you feel disempowered. When another person, most often the parent or the manager, notices this, they often learn to 'press the right' button to induce that feeling within you. Then, when you react 'guiltily', so to speak, they believe they know how to have power over you.

Once again the Truth can set you Free!
'In truth' neither the images of 'being good' or 'being bad' are the true image/idea of one's self, simply because 'the self' can never be an image/idea! The 'goodness' that is often referred to as conscience or the innate true nature of every human being, has no opposite. There are only 'degrees of alignment' or misalignment with the inherent 'trueness' of our nature. In reality, the true self is 'prior to' any and all mental images, therefore prior to the 'ideas' of good and bad, and therefore prior to the judgments of 'right' and

'wrong'. The true self has no image and is not an idea, and is beyond the duality of all concepts.

Here is where things get a little tricky or subtle. In the universe of consciousness, there is no right and wrong! It's hard to see this because we have been so deeply conditioned to 'believe' in right and wrong. It's as if we have been programmed to judge others and our own actions as right or wrong, and therefore good and bad. But the ideas of right and wrong are simply functions of 'duality', which is a condition of the outer material world. Consciousness itself is prior to this duality. There are no opposites in consciousness. And consciousness is what we are.

Being Nudged into Alignment

Our 'conscience' is therefore our innate awareness of what is true which, in the context of our self, is being our 'true self'. Not truth in an absolute and philosophically definable sense, but truth in the sense that a compass is always pointing to 'true north', no matter where in the world it may be. Our 'trueness' is our true nature which is peaceful, loving and joyful. Conscience is our compass and it always points us toward our 'true north'. It's function is to nudge us and let us know when we have created thought and action that is out of alignment with our 'trueness', out of alignment with our true nature which is peaceful, loving and joyful. Unfortunately, influenced by the viral beliefs mentioned here, we get into the habit of ignoring and even suppressing its 'nudges'.

From a purely spiritual point of view conscience is the eternal, unchanging, true state of the energy of the self. It's that 'still core' of our being that is untouched by anything. As soon as we use our energy in a way that contradicts or disturbs that vibration, it sends us a subtle message. We then either listen to that message and allow it to guide us back into alignment or we ignore and suppress it. Like the carpenter who goes against the grain of the wood, he immediately notices how much harder it is to shape the wood and how the wood becomes rougher as a result. When we go against the grain of our conscience, when we don't follow its guidance, when we ignore its quiet voice and subtle feeling that this action or that action was against the grain of our truth (true vibration), we get a signal. We feel a moment of discomfort.

Signals from the Deep

There is no opposite to this 'trueness', this true vibration at our core, only degrees of misalignment, only shades of obscurity clouding our ability to be aware of where the compass of our conscience is pointing us. That obscurity is often called our 'desires'. A strong desire will often make us compromise our self i.e. ignore the guiding nudges of conscience. For example, the desire for some form of personal, physical pleasure may crowd out the inner signal to give time and attention to helping someone in need. From deep within there might emerge a subtle feeling from our conscience signaling us to review our decision.

The signals from our conscience are also distorted by our emotions. We all know that when we are emotional in any way, it's harder to hear and be guided by our conscience, by the true vibration of our consciousness. We often ignore such signals in favor of experiencing some pleasurable emotion which we have not yet realized is a form of dis - ease. For example, when we seek excitement, believing it to be happiness, it sabotages our ability to decide in favor of using our time more wisely or more creatively as we prefer to seek a quick thrill. From within our consciousness, our conscience will draw our attention to our impatience and perhaps our selfishness indicating they are out of alignment with our true nature which is loving i.e. selfless and patient. If we continue our inner enquiry towards where the nudges of conscience are pointing us, we may even realise a basic mistake. We are confusing excitement with happiness. In reality excitement is just stimulation.

How Conscience is Ignored

In the world 'out there' (in society), stealing is seen as something wrong and therefore bad. Society has to consider it so at this time otherwise there would be chaos. But in the context of the world 'in here', within our consciousness, the intention to steal and covet is not wrong as opposed to right. It is simply an act that is out of alignment with our truth or our true nature. We innately know that in order to sustain harmonious relationships with others and the world around us, stealing is not an option. So what then is 'the truth' in the case of stealing? What is the truth 'in here' when any of us steals anything 'out there'? We temporarily lose our ability to hear and feel that inner voice which is guiding us to act in an 'accurate' way, a non-stealing way, because we are 'distracted'!

What do we mean by 'distracted'? Imagine you are ending another day and heading for bed. You walk around the house to lock up. You are passing through the kitchen on your way to your bedroom. But there, on the kitchen table, is a plate and on the plate is a slice of your all-time favorite chocolate cake. Your mind says, "That plate should be cleaned and put back in the cupboard!" Which is code for, "I would like to eat that cake!" So you stop and eat the cake. Which is, of course, extremely nice! You wash the plate and place it in the cupboard. But on your way upstairs a little voice in your head whispers, "I wonder if that cake was for someone else in the house. Perhaps they had just gone somewhere and were on their way back to have their cake."

You were 'distracted' away from doing the accurate thing (keep walking to your bed) by the cake and your desire to taste chocolate (pleasurable stimulation)!

Distracted by our Beliefs

When we act against our conscience, against our innate awareness of what would be the truest action, the accurate action, it's always because we are distracted within our consciousness by the presence of 'belief'. Our beliefs are the equivalent of the cake on the way to bed, but not quite as tasty! There are usually three reasons why people steal, three beliefs within their consciousness that 'distract' them from deciding to do that which is aligned with their trueness: a) they believe that if they can have the object that they covet, it will in some way complete them, b) they believe that when they get what they covet, it will make them happy, c) they believe that they can possess the object. All these beliefs are not 'true' within the universe of the self or consciousness.

What might be called 'spiritual truths', or just 'truths', in this example are: a) we are already complete and that completeness can never be lost, but we may temporarily lose our 'awareness' of it, b) no material object can give us authentic happiness, only a temporary stimulation, because authentic happiness truly comes from inside out, c) as we have already explored, at the level of our 'consciousness', there is a truth that reminds us that, in reality, it's impossible to 'possess' anything.

These are not easy insights (truths) to grasp, as they are not factored into our childhood education. They are spiritual truths that live quietly within our being. Not as intellectual ideas, but as states of being, which if compromised will trigger our conscience to send us a signal. Unfortunately, the 'beliefs' that acquiring things brings completeness, happiness, fulfillment etc., are given to us as truths at a young age. Hence our confusion when we do get what we want and we still feel incomplete, still feel unhappy, and live in fear of losing what we mistakenly think we now possess!

So, in truth, when we steal it's not BAD or WRONG as opposed to GOOD and RIGHT. It's just that we have lost our awareness of our truth (true nature) and we are therefore acting out of alignment with our truth (true nature). If we do steal, our conscience will nudge us. Not because it's wrong or bad, it is trying to remind us that we are acting out of alignment with our true nature, not because society says so, but because we are denying and suppressing the truth of who we are as complete, free, already contented beings.

Our conscience is not telling us that we have 'done wrong' and that we 'are bad'. Those are just previously learned 'viral beliefs' that are triggered. Our conscience is signaling to us that we have fallen under the 'illusion' that we are incomplete, unhappy and unfulfilled. But we ignore and even suppress this signal, this message, from the heart of our being, especially if everyone else around us is doing so. Unfortunately, many have now learned to suppress their conscience and, distracted by those and many other viral beliefs, are acting out of alignment with their trueness. Which is why society has to make laws to keep huge numbers from stealing. If we were all guided by our conscience (our trueness), then societal laws would be unnecessary.

In some ways, this can sound like permission to go and do anything we like, but that's not the key inference here. There are already enough people doing that anyway, despite the laws of the land attempting to define what is right and wrong and therefore good and bad. The inference here is that every human being has a conscience. Everyone has an innate awareness of how to live and create actions that are accurately aligned with their true nature which is loving and peaceful.

Light Bulb Moments

Let's return to our light bulb illuminating a room. The room is filled with sensors. If the light of the bulb fluctuates and dims below a certain intensity/brightness, the sensors will go off. The room is a metaphor for our consciousness. The light is what we are. If something like a belief or a desire obscures our light or distorts our light and starts to compromise the radiance of our true nature which is peaceful and loving, our conscience will send us a message usually in the form of a feeling. It is letting us know that we are thinking and acting out of alignment with our trueness. The curtains of belief, the distractions of desire, the attachment to images in our mind, all serve to dim the true brightness of the light of our consciousness. They veil the heart of our consciousness which we call 'conscience.' But when we are in that state of our true brightness, when nothing is blocking, distorting or distracting the radiance of our consciousness, there is no thought of doing anything that would be out of alignment with that state.

Reawakening Consciousness and Conscience

In some cultures, there seems to be a new generation that is growing up with almost no idea of how to live in harmony with others within society and even within their own family. Their actions seem to come from a violent inner space in such a way that they seem to have no conscience. They seem to have no inner guidance that they are thinking and acting 'inaccurately', that they are out of harmony with everything within themselves and with everyone outside themselves. These youths have been deemed to be hopeless cases by many and, in some places, efforts to help them have been abandoned. They have been irrevocably labeled as 'bad people' to such an extent the term 'feral' has been used to describe them. Unfortunately, when they get that label they tend to accept it, identify with it and therefore live up to it!

However, there are a growing number of cases where such youths have been redeemed, where their conscience has been brought back to life. This seems to happen only when they receive intense personal mentoring by one other person. The role of the mentor is simple - to give them unconditional regard and respect as human beings, regardless of their past, their behavior in the present or their intentions for the future. Slowly, but surely, over time, the suppressed, distorted and distracted light of their conscience, their 'trueness', begins to re-awaken and guide their thoughts, decisions and actions.

Not because they are told what is right and wrong by an outside force, not because they learn to believe in good over bad, but through the gradual realization of how to live in alignment with their own 'inner light'. They restore their capacity to live with honesty and integrity, and thereby integrate harmoniously within the context of their relationships. Their true nature, their 'trueness', is redeemed. It's a good example of how the true nature of human consciousness is always there 'prior to' and beneath the many layers of beliefs, negative self images and memories of painful experiences that can suppress the light of our 'trueness'.

Being Guided by our Truth
So it appears that the 'truth guide' of human consciousness known as 'conscience' never dies, but its guidance is either ignored, suppressed, distracted or distorted. It's hard for many to see and accept that. They have such a deep attachment to a particularly strong belief that human beings can be innately, naturally bad, vile and malevolent without the possibility of redemption. We each have to decide for our self. It is a key decision, as it will affect our vision of

'the other' and therefore our relationships with others in significant ways.

But if it is true that all people have an innate 'light' of truth within them, then it means there are no bad people, only unaware, forgetful, misled people, whose conscience is temporarily disconnected, whose light is temporarily dimmed. This understanding frees us from judging, labeling and condemning others with the 'you are a bad person' label. It helps to release us from our own self-imposed self-image based on the 'I am a bad person' label. It ultimately frees us from that debilitating emotional matrix we know as 'guilt'. It may even help propel us into a more enlightened state where one of the primary realizations is that 'in reality' there are no bad human beings.

That's not so easy if we still rely on Hollywood and Bollywood to role model and glamorize human characters with a suppressed and distorted conscience as our heroes! After a lifetime of conditioning and cultivating the mental habit of judging, after years of being exposed to the judgments of others, after absorbing so many media perceptions that many people are just plain evil and irredeemable, after a lifetime of conditioned thinking in terms of 'good' and 'bad', holding the recognition that there are no bad people is not such an easy 'inner space' to be in and live from. Then again, perhaps it is just what the world now awaits.

Finally, for a future Cappuccino Conversation!
Once we are **aware** of the presence of guilt, the healing of this crippling dis - ease of the soul can only happen when we **realize**, "I am and you are neither good nor bad, neither right or wrong...ever! " We are either awake and aware at the deepest level of our being, where there is no good/bad or right/wrong, simply our true state, our 'trueness'. Or...we're not! Discuss!

Reflections for your journal

Awareness: Take a moment and identify the last two occasions when you felt guilty about something. Note down the thoughts you created in those moments.

Realization: Articulate the belief behind those thoughts that you were holding in those moments. What would be the underlying truth that would set you free?

Transformation: The next time you are in similar situations with the same people what would you say or do differently as you act from that truth.

8

"Oh no, not them again!"

The Dis - Ease of ALLERGY

There is a Dis - ease of consciousness known as ALLERGY. It tends to happen in one or more of our relationships where 'the other' is someone whom we just don't get on with. There is either a clash of personalities or what seems to be an instant, unexplainable dislike. The main symptom is a strong RESISTANT REACTION to the other person. Sometimes there seems to be no clear reason for what is usually mutual. At other times, we know exactly why we become prickly in 'their' presence. The 'viral beliefs' are not so easy to see, but one of them usually sounds something like, "I'll never get on with them." Perhaps that's the mild version! Other arising beliefs and thoughts include, "They just rub me up the wrong way," which is usually code for, "They shouldn't be like the way they are, they should be more like...me!"

What we don't notice is they are usually mirroring something within our self that we can't or don't want to see and acknowledge. While we may say that we are not threatened by 'them', subconsciously we are. While we may even try to disguise our discomfort in their presence, ultimately we are writhing in a kind of emotionally suppressed agony. If our consciousness could come out in a rash, in such moments we would be scratching our self silly! We want them to go away, however, like any itchy rash, the more you scratch, the more it itches. In relational terms, this means the more you resist them, the more frequently they 'seem' to turn up and the stronger our resistance/reaction becomes.

Vive La Difference

This is one of the toughest dis - eases of the soul to heal. Simply because there are so many subtle 'viral beliefs' that we are holding about the other, both consciously and subconsciously. Ultimately, there has to be a shift from resistance to acceptance in our heart and mind if we are to free our self from our emotional discomforts around 'them'. This is helped, but not cured, by the realization of one basic truth; that every single human being is unique and different, and therefore each one must inevitably create a different personality.

If we can acknowledge, celebrate and appreciate our own uniqueness, it becomes easier to accept and celebrate others, instead of resenting the way they are. If we can value and appreciate variety, not only in a box of chocolates, but in all human relationships, we may eventually grow and step beyond the feeling of having to 'tolerate' them and into a heart-felt celebration of their presence in our life.

In the meantime, it's useful to refine our own awareness of why we may be allergic to some people and not others. Why do some people seem to make us itch more than others?

The Relationship has a Back Story!

Sometimes, there is a history to our difficult and allergic relationship with this particular person. Usually the story contains moments when we believed they did or said something that hurt our feelings. That usually translates into our fear that it may happen again. So we find our self 'on edge' in their company. Only the realization, that no-one ever 'hurts' our feelings and that we are the creator of all our emotional suffering, can eventually set us free enough to relax into the relationship.

An Uncomfortable Reminder

Sometimes one particular person simply reminds us of someone else we have known in the past whom we believe wronged us or hurt us. The person to whom we are highly allergic in the present is unknowingly pressing a subconscious button within us that is reactivating the memory of the suffering. That's what is making us resist them, avoid them and even project on to them blame for other current miseries in our life. Once again, realizing the truth that we are self-responsible, that any mental or emotional suffering in the past was our own creation, can start to set us free and empower us not to resist or react to this person.

Consciously or Subconsciously Jealous

Sometimes we clash with someone because there is something within their personality that we believe we should have. Behind our behavior there is a jealousy that is poisoning the relationship. Even though we may be good at disguising it, even though we ourselves cannot see it clearly, there is a subtle jealousy there. It distorts our ability to accept that the other has a quality, perhaps a presence, a unique capacity, that we can appreciate and not be envious of. Our inability to extend appreciation to another is a sign that we have not yet realized one of the most powerful truths of human relationships. When you 'appreciate' a virtue or attribute of another's character, in that moment you start to nurture and grow that same virtue or attribute within your own character!

Mirror Mirror - Who is Not the Fairest of Us All?

Sometimes someone is simply just a powerful mirror for some not so pleasant trait or tendency that we have developed. But we just don't want to see and acknowledge it. Our way of avoiding it is to attack the other with some not-so-nice beliefs about 'them'. When we think or say something about them, we don't notice our contradiction and our hypocrisy. We don't want to face it. "They shouldn't be so critical all the time," is a moment when we just don't notice we ourselves are being critical almost all the time... about them!

Position and not the Person

Sometimes, especially in the workplace, we find our self allergic to someone in authority. In such instances, it usually means we are having a relationship with a position and not the person. We see them as their position, which means we are seeing our self as a position, in relation to them. Which is not true. No-one is a position! Only when we start to appreciate the other as human being and stop seeing them as someone who has positional power over us will things settle down. Only then will the animosity and resentment, that is usually behind our allergic reactions, start to disappear.

It's not hard to spot the symptoms of this dis - ease of the soul that can be likened to a kind of allergy. You will notice these symptoms whenever you become **aware** of your resistance towards another. That can take the form of any emotional reaction towards the other, outright mental rejection of the other or the more subtle ways in which we use to avoid the other.

There are many realizations which can signal the curing of your allergy to either one person or to all those that you have previously shunned. Perhaps the first is the insight into the nature of the actual energetic exchange that is relationship.

It's a **realization** that paves the way to an ability to not only welcome those whom you would have resisted, but to celebrate their presence in your life. And it sounds like this, "It's not what you say or do that makes me feel this way, it's what I do with what you say or do that makes me feel this way." This the realization that it's the way in which we are creating the other within our consciousness that is bothering us. It's not the way the person is themselves. This is a prerequisite to the liberating truth that our allergy is not only fixable, but it's healing is a **transformation** that, for some, can finally make life worth living...again.

Understanding the dynamics of the process gets us halfway there. The other half is our responsibility to take full responsibility for our creation. Then we can stop misusing 'them' to bother our self! Then we may realize that the person that we previously considered 'most difficult' turned out to be our best teacher!

Reflective questions for your journal

Awareness: Identify the three people with whom you would say you are most allergic.

Realization: Why do you really think you are allergic to them (maybe different reasons for each one). What are the beliefs that you are holding about each one that is making you resist them or react to their presence?

Transformation: Looking at each one individually, what truth about them would start to set you free of the allergy and allow to connect with them with greater comfort and ease?

9

"Wait till I tell them!"

The Dis - Ease of INCONTINENCE

There is a Dis - Ease that can develop within consciousness known as INCONTINENCE. The primary symptoms are non-stop thinking and talking, and/or needing to be always seen as the one who is doing the thinking and talking! Usually it's both! The 'viral belief' that lies behind this dis - ease is often a deep subconscious belief that, "I need to be affirmed by others." Some of the arising thoughts that are symptomatic of incontinence of the soul will probably include, "I need to tell them..." "They need to know...", or "Wait till I tell ..." or "They'll never believe...". Often there are no such precise thoughts preceding the words of the incontinent as everything just spills out uncontrollably anyway!

The 'incontinent consciousness' will usually be in a state of expansion and speculation about many things. The actual conversations when the incontinent does let rip are likely to be motivated by three forms of neediness. The first is the need to be the centre of attention. The second is the need to be recognised, validated and valued as the one 'who is in the know'. The third need is often to release and relieve themselves of the mental pressure from so much thinking, evaluating, judging, speculating, interpreting, concluding, surmising, correcting ...phew!

Just as the physical dysfunction we know as incontinence is difficult to cure, so the dis - ease of the incontinence of consciousness is hard to heal. Within its process, there seems to be so many moments of apparent pleasure. "Oooo...you mean you didn't know...!" "I never thought I would be the one to tell you...!" "I am so glad you like my interpretation of what is going on with them...!"

Being listened to intently, being validated and valued as the one who knows is an addiction to a 'fix' that's hard to fix! Exhaustion slows things down, but it's not a fix. The shock, that the 'loose talk' can have the effect of triggering an unfortunate turn of events in someone else's life, may make the 'incontinent' hesitate a little in their uncontrolled blathering. But probably not for very long. Someone else may give them some feedback about their incessant yakking that triggers them to take a closer look at themselves. But the incontinent is good at finding justification for their unsolicited, attention-seeking, needy ramblings.

The realization that in their busy-ness with other people's business, "I am missing my own life," may or may not occur. If it does, it can signal a major shift in attention and energy. Ultimately however, there has to be a deep recognition that their neediness to be heard by others, for the validation of others, to be valued by others, can only ever be assuaged by their own self realization of their true value. It's only when they realize that their sense of worth and worthiness is sourced, seen and known from within, that the busy-body, busy-mind and busy-tongued habits can be...cured!

The Blather of Discontentment

Yet, even that's probably not possible until there is a 'reversal of intention' from wanting to giving. In their incontinence, they seem to be giving and they themselves believe they are giving, but in reality they are wanting and taking. It's only when we give of our self without desire that we come to know what we are and the value of what we have within us. The challenge for those afflicted by incontinence of the soul is to realize they are not really 'giving' anything when they are mentally or verbally spilling the beans. They are wanting attention and taking validation from whoever will listen to them. Even if there isn't anyone around, they will likely blather silently to imagined others in their own heads.

It's only in the process of genuinely giving of themselves, free of wanting anything in return, that they may realize they don't need anything from anyone. Yes, as we explored earlier, our body needs food, shelter, clothing etc. But the 'I', the me, the self, needs nothing. When that is realized, it becomes easy to sit quietly, even silently, free of needing to be listened to, affirmed, valued or even acknowledged by others. The strength and the value of the self is known directly from within in a way that all 'neediness', all desire for anything from others, dissolves. In many ways, this is one of the deepest freedoms.

It's about Love Actually!

One of the most powerful realizations can happen at any time. It's normally happens during the process of being loving towards another. It is the 'love is what I am' AHA moment! In such moments the self realizes that, "What I previously believed I needed, I don't!" It's already present. This realization 'can' wipe out all further searching for love in the forms of recognition, approval and validation from others or from the world. At least for some it can. For others it's not so easy to allow such a realisation to be fully integrated. It is not helped when everyone else around us is still in the 'searching for love' mode. This belief, that love must be sought from others, is so deep and shared by so many, it sits at the heart of modern culture. Even when there has been the realization that love is ultimately what I am, that I now know my value as a source of love, it's still not easy to free oneself from the 'neediness and seeking habits'.

If that realization is authentic, if the freedom from needing anything intangible from others is authentic, then a quiet contentment begins to arise from within. You will notice a sense of completeness replaces the neediness that was coming from an illusory sense of emptiness. The blethering subsides, replaced by a vibration of tranquility that radiates outwards. You are then able to hear others at a deeper level. They will feel they are receiving something of great value simply through the attentiveness of your compassionate listening.

Yes sometimes, we do need to express our self, to say something, to share something, but when it doesn't come from a place of need it is more like a gift given. The feelings of dis - ease, that arise and move us to babble on, have gone. In their place is a sensitivity to others' communication and a clear sense of when it is appropriate to make your contribution to the conversation. That's when others are drawn towards your ease and they are no longer concerned with either avoiding or being overwhelmed by your incontinental dis - ease!

In summary, the curing of this form of soul dis - ease starts when we become **aware** that the yabber, yabber and more yabber has its origins in a mind that just cannot sit still, that must always be thinking about others and is continuously mentally, if not verbally, talking to others, usually about others. This outpouring of mental energy frequently manifests itself in an avalanche of words in one-way conversations. **Realization** begins when we see there is a deep sense of insecurity within the self about one's own validity and worth. All because of a 'viral belief' that says our existence has to be acknowledged and valued by others before we can feel alive and enjoy our life. The cure has started to 'kick in' when there is the realization that others can never give us what is already within i.e. our own sense of value and worth. We only need to realize the truth of what we are, of who the 'I' that says, "I am," actually is. It's only when we realize that we are seeking from others what we already have within our own being that it's possible to end the habit of wanting and seeking the validation of others. The **transformation** is complete when we are able to sit and both listen and speak from a quiet contentment, where before an excitable agitation would have had us hijacking the conversation with mostly trivial, if not completely irrelevant, information.

Reflections for your journal

Awareness: On a scale of one to a hundred (1 is low 100 is high) where would you rate your level of incontinence?

Realization: Why exactly do you think you sometimes just blather on when you have your attacks of verbal incontinence? What are you seeking?

Transformation: Consciously practice being quietly content in all your conversations this week.

10

"I need to know more!"

The Dis - Ease of INDIGESTION

There is a Dis - ease of consciousness known as INDIGESTION. The primary symptoms are mental confusion, the inability to focus attention, occasional storms of emotional agitation with outbreaks of florid language interspersed with verbal and social constipation! The viral belief that causes this disease is, "I need to know what's going on." The arising thoughts include, "I may miss something important" or "I wonder what happened to..." or "I need to know more about..." or "I am sure there is something new that I may have missed..."

When we eat too much too fast, our physical digestive system can't cope. We may suffer anything from acid reflux to gastritis, from bloating to burping, from diarrhea to constipation. Our bodies are telling us to slow down and eat less, to chew our soup and drink our food, as they say!

In the information age, where we now have instant access to just about any subject, any event and the life of almost any person, some of us have developed the tendency to hoover up massive amounts of images, ideas and gossip. We can easily spend all day scanning for news, views and the latest interviews. Just as the food addict fears missing a good snack, some people become agitated when they are cut off from the streams of information that satisfies an incessant addiction to know what's going on in other people's lives. The rainbow of symptoms of this dis - ease within the soul will range from confusion to exhaustion, from excited elation to disappointment, from restlessness to craving. It's the craving for information that pulls us to a screen and a keyboard, at our desk, in our bag or in our pocket, many times every day.

You can observe this almost everywhere, almost every day with almost everyone. Groups of people meet for coffee, but the conversation is delayed as they sit around the table together all checking their smart phones for messages. Teenagers on a mountain trek are oblivious to the spectacular scenery as they all sit around on boulders checking in to see 'what's happening' on their Facebook page. People sitting in the art gallery, surrounded by the most exquisite art, are checking their emails and pouring over photos sent by friends. The delegates attending an expensive and content-rich seminar look up to listen only occasionally from their smart phones under the desk, as they check in with the office and reply to their clients and colleagues as if every message is an emergency. Perhaps this is why Einstein apparently said, "I fear the day that technology will surpass our human interaction. The world will have a generation of idiots."

Being Plugged Out!
And the cure? It's a tough one. Being online used to be about being more 'in contact' with a few others, perhaps connecting with family or friends with the occasional email. It gave us the facility to extend care from a distance, to be in touch quickly in ways that sustained a valuable relationship. It also allowed us to nurture a connection with the larger human family. But being 'online' today, for an increasing number of people, is like inserting an intravenous drip directly into

their minds. If there is a sudden ending of a 'live feed' of the news, of the viral beliefs of others, of the hyper stimulation of 'what's up' from every corner of the world - well, for those who have reached a highly addictive state, withdrawing that drip can be the equivalent of extremely cold turkey! Being 'plugged out' for them is a frightening thought.

Need to Know Less

One frank admission and one significant recognition are signs that the immune systems healing power has begun its work. First some honesty and the admission, "Yes I am an addict, I'm an 'infoholic! I am a technoholic! I do suffer from 'info indigestion." Second, the recognition, "I don't 'need to know what's going on more than three feet away from me 95% of the time."

What can help to sustain the realization of these two 'realities' is when we look back over an average day and ask our self how much of the information that we consumed can we remember. Usually very little! Probably less than 5%. Why? Because it had no real value. It was the equivalent of junk food. There was little or no real mental or intellectual nourishment. We just didn't need to know it, we just didn't need to consume it.

Real Nourishment

So what does nourish us? What is a healthy source of information that is also of value to us and may even strengthen us? It's the information that arises in the process of self reflection. It comes from 'inside out' and not 'outside in'. It's information about what we are feeling, where our thoughts are coming from, what is influencing us to behave the way we do, why we are reacting emotionally and not responding rationally. Cultivating this kind of self-informed understanding is at the heart of the process of healing all the dis - eases featured here. It is enhanced with the practice of meditation, as meditation by definition cultivates, expands and deepens self-awareness. Meditation is the journey away from our addiction to information, replacing it with a reconnection to our own innate wisdom.

Realizing Reality

Another insight or truth that may help set you free of the dis - ease known as 'indigestion of the soul' is that you can never miss anything real! What you are consuming electronically is not real. Surfing the digital ocean of life is a somewhat superficial activity. That's fairly obvious. But the idea that you are consuming what is 'unreal' is little more challenging to see. Whatever information you consume after it arrives through your electronic windows onto the world has been filtered and interpreted by other people's intellects. It is re-presented and re-shaped by the nature of the electronic medium itself. It is decontextualised and magnified, glamorized and repackaged for our thirsty ego! So it's not real. You are not witnessing reality. It's all artificially molded, morphed, skewed, reconstituted and re-presented in order to keep you interested, hooked, dependent and wanting more. It's designed to encourage you to sustain your habit of investing your sense of identity in other people's lives, in short, to live your life vicariously! That's what it means to live in an 'unreal world'. Unfortunately, it seems to be a world into which more of us are sleepwalking.

So are you going to live in the real, natural world or the unreal manufactured world of others? Try a few days without any technological connectivity whatsoever. The first day will be cold turkey, the second day will bring a stability of mind and a restfulness of heart that reminds you what life used to be like in a slower lane. On the third day, you may realize how much the quality of your mental diet is vital to your well-being. The fourth day could be the beginning of a new habit as you thoughtfully consider everything a little more deeply for your self. You will start 'feel' everything more deeply within your self. You will begin to choose and feel your own 'ease' at will. Well, OK, perhaps four days is a little optimistic!

But do watch for the symptoms of the dis - ease of the soul that could be called 'indigestion'. Your immune system may even jump start itself. It will remind you that most of the information that you consume has little value. You will likely realise that information is at the end of a trail that started with 'truth'. Then truth, through application, became wisdom, which was then crystallized into knowledge. We then used our knowledge to create the technology to generate and ship massive amounts of information across vast distances at lightening speeds! With each transition, some would say fall, the quality of our mental and intellectual diet was diminished, and wellness was lost.

Creating Nutritional Value for the Soul

Next time you are **aware** of a certain dis - ease in relation to the day's news or what seems to be happening in other people's lives, remind yourself that we just don't need to know more than a few percent of what we 'believe' we should and could know. It's that 'viral belief' that says 'I need to know' that causes the eventual reflux of the indigestible information that we call news and other people's views. See if you can **realize** it's ultimately not real and offers no nutritional value to the soul. See 'the real' with your inner eye. Reality is you, the 'I' that says "I am." What is 'real' are the thoughts and feelings that you create. The 'real' is what you are giving to the world, not what you are consuming from the world. Reality is what you hear from your own intuition not what is produced and broadcast by institutions.

Watch for the signs that the healing of your spiritual indigestion is happening and that **transformation** has begun. You tap on a keyboard once an hour, not five times an hour. You check your phone for messages once an hour not ten times an hour. You can be frequently seen staring out the window into the infinity of outer space as you contemplate and ruminate on possibilities, on ideas, on insights, that you are creating and 'playing' with in the primary and infinite reality of your own consciousness.

Awareness: How frequently do you find your self consuming information each day - try to pin it down to average minutes per hour! Then add it up for a day. Why are you so frequently consuming so much information?

Realization: What percentage of the information is useful, what percentage is nourishing you, what percentage is a waste of time and energy?

Transformation: Create five alternative 'creative actions' i.e. things you can do instead of consuming information from the electronic media. In other words, it's not that you stop using electronic media as a resource, but what could be dropped and replaced by your own creativity?

11

"I am always right"

The Dis - Ease of ARTHRITIS

There is a dis - ease of consciousness which could be called 'arthritis of the soul'! It's primary symptom is a deep inflexibility that borders on chronic rigidity. The underlying 'viral belief' is, "I am right about everything." Arising thoughts sound like, "This is the way I see it and it's the only right way to see it...!" "There is only one right way to do this and that's the way I do it...!"

Like its physical equivalent, where there is a painful stiffness of the body's joints, there is a stiffness in the soul that shows up as a closed attitude to new ways of seeing and doing. While there is pain when a physical joint which is arthritic is made to bend, with 'arthritis of the soul' there is suffering in the unbending resistance to the ideas and ways of others. That suffering is obviously emotional and it shows up as a swing between anger as in, "How dare they try to make me see it or do it differently," and/or fear as in, "This can't go on can it and/or surely they could not be more right than me!"

The arthritic soul has rigid opinions and usually holds fast to a set of beliefs assimilated and formed a long time in the past. Deeply religious people tend to suffer from spiritual arthritis. Their sense of identity, security and stability is based on their religious beliefs absorbed from ancient scripture or others interpretations of those scriptures. Having 'adopted' those beliefs they will eventually consider their beliefs to be their own personal truths. They will seldom have stopped to explore and understand the difference between belief and truth. Yet, it's only with the lubrication of new insights, new ways of perceiving, new ways of understanding one's self, new ways of making meaning in day-to-day living, that new truths can be realised and old beliefs released. It's only the continuous realisation of new truths that will eventually provide the arthritic soul with relief from the self-created suffering that arises from rigidly holding fast to one set of beliefs.

This is why the primary difference between religion and spirituality is often the difference between belief and truth. Religion tends to say you 'must believe' what you have been told or there will be dire consequences. Spirituality tends to say believe nothing and by using a particular practice you may see and realise what is true for your self. Religion tends to say 'belief' is enough whereas spirituality would say belief is, at best, a signpost and at worst, a blindfold. Belief tends to come from 'outside in' where as 'realised truth' comes from inside out. Belief is confined by ideas and concepts whereas the truth is more like a multidimensional state of being with infnite depth. As an everyday example, to look at your business card and 'believe' you are what it says on the card is not true. Few realise that the truth starts with 'I am not what I do' and ends with I am the 'I' that says, "I am", that's all!

A Dark Grumpiness
It's probably true to say that most of us grow up with the dis - ease of arthritis growing within us. Simply because we blindly believe what we are taught or told by those big people called parents and teachers. So often in workshops and seminars, I encounter people with different forms of

arthritis of the soul. The most common seem to be the ones who tend to sit with arms tightly folded across their chest. Their facial expression tends toward a dark grumpiness. The vibration emanating from them seems to be saying, "I really don't want to be here." After a while and out of an obviously growing frustration, they put their hand up and start to complain that they just don't agree. They start to tell me, in no uncertain terms, their own beliefs, in a tone that says they are feeling very uncomfortable and resistant to the point of view they are perceiving in what I am saying. At which point, I usually say (and I should also say this here in the context this book, just in case you are feeling a little arthritic in response to some of the content!), "Please don't believe a word I say, I am not here to convince you of anything. I am just rambling on and, in doing so, describing what I see when I explore these issues/subjects etc. for myself within my self! My views/insights/realizations may change next week or next year. Indeed I hope they do. I hope they become deeper and feel even more aligned to what is true for me. But please don't just believe what I say otherwise you may miss seeing something fresh and new for your self. And that is why we are all here right now, to see and realize for ourselves what is true today and not so much what is just another assimilated belief from yesterday."

Just a little!

At this point, they usually relax ...a little. They become more receptive, well ... a little! The eye of their intellect opens ... a little more. The egoless state known as 'curiosity' expands ...a little! The arthritic joints between their joined-up belief systems seem to loosen and become less painful...a little! They are able to bend a little more easily and they do, sometimes even with a smile and a 'thank you.' But who knows for how long.

Tough to Cure

We already know that arthritis of the body is not easy to treat. Similarly, arthritis of the soul is tough to cure. It becomes harder to see that, just as diet is huge factor in physical arthritis, our mental and intellectual diet in the past has been a huge factor in our spiritual arthritis in the present. Once again it's the ego that's at work here, as it ultimately is with all these dis - eases. The arthritic soul is simply consciously and subconsciously attached to, and identifying themselves with, their beliefs. Hence the creation of the ego. They become trapped in the forms that their beliefs take within their mind. It's as if they become their beliefs. This is like your body thinking it is the chair it's sitting in. If your body could think that, and if it did think that, your body would never walk again. Your body, with you in it, would be permanently stuck in the chair. And that's why arthritis of the soul feels and looks like a kind of permanently fixed viewpoint, with rigid perceptions and frozen interpretations that just repeat themselves. It all adds up to a stuck attitude that generates repetitive behavior patterns.

Relief comes when the arthritic soul awakens and becomes **aware** of the value of one of three things; learning from others, understanding the other and being a guide for others. When they engage in any of these interactivities, they will naturally start to loosen their grasp on their rigid thinking and fixed believing. They naturally **realize** there are more valid angles, more varied points of view, more options to move forwards than they had previously conceived. That kind of realization leads naturally to **transformation** as the previously arthritic soul ceases to trap themselves in, and be shaped by, the same old 'chair of beliefs'. They stand up and it's as if their spirit starts dancing with new ways of seeing, new insights into knowing, as they reinvigorate deeper levels of their own being. Sometimes the transformation of the arthritic soul is signaled by a return to a childlike enthusiasm. It's as if they are discovering the world all over again. There is an 'intoxication of spirit' as consciousness breathes in and out the fresh and invigorating air of new realizations, insights, and understanding.

It's no small acheivement to go from your chair to the dance floor after years of arthritis. It's worth celebrating when someone does get up and starts 'movin and shakin' their old joints! If you are ever in the room when this happens to someone, feel privileged to be present. You are probably watching what is sometimes called a minor miracle. It's an equally joyful moment when someone starts to drop their rigidly held views and opinions, beliefs and behaviours. Those around them start to say or think things like, "Wow! You really have changed. You really are more flexible and easy to be with. You really are...well!"

If you think you are someone with a few painfully stiff and swollen 'spiritual joints', call your local dance instructor now!

Reflections for your journal

Awareness: When do you find your self resisting the ideas and opinions of others the most? What are the beliefs that you notice in such situations that you are rigidly holding on to? Why do you think that is?

Realization: What is the difference between belief and truth - research and investigate. Note down your realizations on the way.

Transformation: What differences in attitudes and behaviors would people see and feel from you if you were more open and flexible?

12

"I can't do love, it's just not me!"

The Dis - Ease of Asthma

There is a dis - ease of consciousness which could be known as ASTHMA of the soul. The primary symptom is the inability to 'express love'. While diabetes of the soul is the incapacity to receive, accept and assimilate love from others, so asthma is the sign of a soul that finds it hard to give love and be loveful anytime, anywhere. They may believe they are 'giving' but it's usually not with their heart and more from the head.

Someone having a 'physical asthma attack' finds it hard to 'breath in' air. Something is constricting and narrowing their airways. Someone having a 'spiritual asthma attack' finds it almost impossible to 'breathe out' their love towards others. Something is constricting their heart and the pathway from their heart to 'the other'. Not the heart of their body but the heart of their being.

In a physical asthma attack, the bands of muscle surrounding the airways tighten. The lining of the airways become swollen and inflamed. The cells that line the airways produce a thicker mucus than normal. In a spiritual asthma attack, the ability to be loving is constricted by the shrinking of the heart's capacity to radiate the energy of love. The inflammation is signaled by the 'emotional mucus' we know as the various forms of fear and anger.

The Oxygen of the Soul

In the physical dimension, air is taken in by the body in order to acquire the life-giving oxygen essential to the health of our body. When there is the in-breath of air, it's not you that is breathing, it's your body! In the spiritual dimension, which is you the consciousness being, love is an outward radiation of the energy of...you! Just as the intake of oxygen is essential to the health of the body, so the radiation of love, is essential to the wellbeing of the soul. When you do anything with love you are essentially giving the energy of you. If you give of your self but still want something in return, your energy becomes distorted and blocked by the idea/image in your mind of what you want. In such moments, you are not a well being because implicit in all desire is fear. Wanting is the conversion of love into fear.

Love is the oxygen of the soul! But the spiritual oxygen of love needs to be radiated and released not acquired and consumed, for wellness to be restored and maintained. This means that the difference between body and soul can be summed up by two dynamics. The body is designed to 'take in' nutrients and oxygen to maintain its health. The soul is designed to 'give out' the energy/vibration of light and love, which are the spiritual nutrients that maintain its wellbeing. The body's nature is to consume and soul's nature is to radiate.

The constriction of the body's airways appear to be 'triggered' (but not caused) by many things such as food, other people, stressful situations, the environment, even the weather.

However the constriction of the radiant energy of the soul is caused by one thing, attachment.

Understanding the Mind

The mind is not the soul, it is not the self. The mind is the faculty of the soul where the soul receives the sights and sounds of the world 'out there', as they come 'in here' through our eyes. We then put them up on the screen of our mind 'in here'. The mind is also where you create thoughts, ideas and images, which you then radiate from 'in here' out into the world 'out there' through your attitudes and actions. Over time, you start to become attached to and trapped in the ideas and images that you create in your mind. Attachment to any idea or image generates fear. That's why fear becomes the main symptom of the dis - ease of the asthmatic. Fear is love distorted by attachment. Fear is the same radiant energy of consciousness as love. But the vibration of that energy is 'distorted' on the way out by the object (image or idea) to which the self has become attached. Hence the many different feelings of fear that we 'insperience' as worry, tension, anxiety, panic etc.

This is easy to verify from personal experience. One minute you are able to be open and loving towards someone, the next minute you create fear and/or anger towards them when they do not do, or say, or be, exactly the way YOU want. If you could be fully aware in that moment, you would notice the vibration of love that you were giving one minute, turns into fear only moments later, because you have an image in your mind of how you would like them to do/say/be. It's as if you 'shrink-wrap' your self in the image/idea on the mind. You 'shrink' to the size of the image and you are 'wrapped' in the image, which means you are attached to the image. You expect them to be the way you have created them in your mind. When they don't live up to that image, when your expectation of them is not fullfilled, it's your attachment to that image that is converting the vibration of your energy from love into fear/anger. Drop the attachment i.e. come out of the image on your mind, and you return naturally to the heart of your being. Then the energy you give is restored to its original and highest vibration that we know as love. But that's not so easy, simply because we are not so aware of this subtle inner dynamic within our consciousness, within our self. This is the dynamic formation of the ego or false sense of self. The ego being the moment you attach to, and lose your sense of identity in, what is not you! This is also why it is impossible to be authentically loving towards another, unless 'you' are detached or non-attached!

Recognizing an Asthma Attack!

Asthma of the soul is even more common than asthma of the body. Anytime you create and feel any 'emotion' (sadness, anger or fear), it means you are having a spiritual asthma attack! There is a constriction in your ability to give with love. In a physical asthma attack, the struggle to inhale is assisted by the use of an 'external inhaler' which delivers certain chemicals to help decongest and deconstrict the airways. In a spiritual asthma attack, we also need assistance as we struggle to 'exhale' the highest energy, known as love, into our relationships. For this we require the help of an 'internal exhaler'!

There are three kinds of 'internal exhalers' that can open up the pathway from the heart of our being and ensure that we restore and radiate the energy of authentic love. The first is the heart itself. At the heart of our being there is an original and eternal unchanging state that can never be lost. Meditation takes you there. That's why the first and vital step in meditation is to 'detach', which means free your self from all attachment to all thoughts, ideas, images, memories etc. Then your natural state of inner peace is restored. It is within that peace that you will feel the pulse of your spiritual heart, which is the 'natural impulse' to give, to connect, to love. Your natural intention is to give of your self with no thought of anything in return. In such a state of consciousness, there is no thought 'about' one's self, there is just 'being' one's self. In that natural state of being you are radiating the highest energy of one's self as love...naturally!.

Keeping Elevated Company

The second 'internal exhaler' is the company of someone who is being loving, who is in that natural loving state just described. This is where things become a little 'interesting'! The other person appears to be external and they are at a physical level, but not so much at a spiritual level. Have you ever felt up-lifted in the presence of someone who is obviously being unconditionally loving towards everyone around them, including you? In such moments, the energy of your consciousness is being pulled up and into 'resonance' with the vibration of their consciousness. It's as if you are being elevated into a higher state of being by their vibration. In such moments while they appear to be 'out there', you are in fact both connected in what you could call a 'soul to soul connection'. It's as if your two spiritual energies become one! Two Is become one I without losing our sense of 'you' and I.

In such moments there is no 'out there' or 'in here'. There is an invisible energetic connection that you and they will 'feel'. Their higher vibration has an magnetic and elevating influence on your consciousness. That's why it's always beneficial to mix with people who are doing their 'inner work' to raise and refine their consciousness. They are in the process of waking up as they shake of all the illusions and false beliefs gathered along the way. They are awakening and empowering their spiritual immune system and healing all these dis - eases as they recover the wellness of the soul. The ultimate state of wellbeing is seen in someone who is able to stablise themselves in a loving state of consciousness at all times and in all places

The Source or Light and Warmth

The third 'internal exhaler' is also neither internal or external. In truth, in the context of consciousness, which is what the 'I' that says, "I am," is, there is no internal and external. As we explored earlier consciousness is not subject to duality, to such separation. This is why the ultimate source of spiritual energy is a mystery to most. But it's 'the source' that is of the greatest assistance in restoring our ability to be who we are, which is love, and to do what we are designed to do, which is love! This source is sometimes referred to as divine energy, or the love of One, or the love of God, or God as love! It doesn't really matter what labels we use. It is the energy of pure love. So how do we connect with the source? How do we draw on the highest level of spiritual energy? Simply be open. That means be attached to nothing and no one, as it's attachment that keeps our consciousness, our heart, our self, closed!

A Day in the Sun

A metaphor helps. You are standing on the earth. There are clouds in the sky. You cannot see or feel the sun directly because of the clouds. In order to feel the warmth of the sun and absorb the light of the sun, both essential to the health of your body, you need to wait for the clouds to disappear or raise your self up above the clouds. And so it is with your consciousness, with you! Right now the vibrational level of the consciousness of most of us is quite low. It ranges accross a spectrum from slightly unloving to highly resentful! We 'feel' those low vibratory states as forms of fear and anger, anxiety and jealousy, sadness and hopelessness etc. The clouds are all the objects, people, beliefs, memories and situations that we create and attach our 'self' to in our own minds. It's our attachments that block out the light from the source. They are like curtains across the window of our consciousness. Beyond the clouds of our attachments there is the 'source energy' that is vibrating at a much higher level. It is the highest vibration of consciousness, of spirit. We call this vibration pure love, divine love. To connect to the 'source energy' we need to rise above our self-manufactured clouds in our consciousness, which just means let go of our attachments. There is no loss in this, just a change of relationship with whatever and whoever is around us in our life. Which means the reality that nothing and no one is 'mine' is fully realised.

As you let go, as you release all your attachments and therefore your dependencies, the vibration of your consciousness becomes refined and elevated. Internally you are liberating your self. This in turn re-opens you, enabling you to receive and 'connect' with that 'source energy'. In such moments you also feel the 'warmth' of that pure love emanating from the source. You may 'feel' what is sometimes referred to as the greatest bliss. In such moments of connection you are touched by the 'light' of a being with a pure awareness. This reawakens your awareness of your authentic and unconditioned self. You 'fully realise' your self to be the spiritual energy that you are! You are not thinking that! In this state of self-realisation there is no thought, there is no need to think. It is a state that also serves to loosen and break all your subtler subconscious attachment to all the 'viral beliefs' we have been exploring here. In some cultures that 'moment of connection' to the source is sometimes called 'yoga', which just means union.

Where there is union there is love and where there is love there will be union.

In summary, be **aware** of your spiritual asthma attacks. Those moments of mental and emotional disturbance. **Realize** it is just the energy of your heart, of you, that starts out as the vibration of love but is distorted by attachment into feelings of sadness, anger or fear. **Transform** your self, which means take off the 'shrink-wrapping' of your attachments. Restore your consciousness to its highest level of vibration and you will naturally connect and resonate with 'the source'. Allow that 'insperience' to **transform** you so that you no longer need to take the form of your attachments. Notice you are and always were a free spirit, in reality! Notice how you can now 'breathe freely' from the heart of you, without constriction or restriction. As you do, you will also notice that you truly are 'well in your being' again.

Reflections for your Journal

Awareness: Look back over the day and pin-point moments when you had a spiritual asthma attack i.e. moments when you became sad, angry or fearful? Note them down.

Realization: What did you want in those moments from the other or from the situation, but believed you were not getting - this could be tangible or intangible?

Transformation: Imagine you knew your role in each of these situations is to be the giver, to be the person whose job it was to bring something valuable, beneficial to the person or situation. What would that be in each situation? Be as specific as possible.

PART THREE

BE Well - STAY Well - GO Well

be·ing
Living; existing, being alive.
Synonyms - existence - life - entity - essence
Synonyms in a purely spiritual context - soul, self, spirit, consciousness, pure awareness.

well·ness
The natural state or condition of being prior to a loss of pure awareness.

Being is Becoming

So now you know, now you are fully aware, if you weren't before, that wellness is a condition of the soul. It is a 'natural state' of the spiritual being that you are. A 'well being' doesn't rest on their laurels. They have a fine-tuned awareness of what is affecting their consciousness on the inside and they have fully realized the truth that no person, event or circumstance, can make them feel unwell. It's always ME that does that!

The 'well being' also integrates daily practices into their life that are vital to the maintenance of their wellness, allowing them to **be well** again after a lifetime of many forms of dis - ease, **stay well** in whatever situation they find themselves and to **go well** wherever in the world they decide to take themselves.

When we find and fix our physical diseases, they usually stay fixed, with a few exceptions perhaps. But with the dis - eases of consciousness, it tends to be the other way round. We often get a quick insight into a truth, which momentarily cancels out the 'viral belief' that is the cause of our dis - ease. There is perhaps a brief transformation of attitude and behavior, a brief relief from an inner discomfort, but then the old belief and the consequent behaviors soon kick back in, unless we are vigilant. The reason is our old friend 'habit'.

Habit Keeps our Dis - eases Alive

We tend to think of habits as physical actions that we do repeatedly. But habits have their origin deep within our consciousness at the level of our beliefs and perceptions, which in turn shape our habitual thoughts and feelings, which then drive our behavior. All these dis - eases of our consciousness tend to become 'layered habits'. Together they make up our comfort zone. That's why most of us learn to be comfortable being uncomfortable, happy being unhappy, and we won't even be aware of it!

Humbled to Our Knees

Although it seems perverse to believe we are happy and comfortable while being somewhat miserable, the vast majority of us do learn to tolerate our 'dis - eases of the soul' until the level of our suffering or unhappiness becomes so intense we are forced to look at it. Only then do we do something about it. Many of us will wait till that moment when we hit rock bottom, the lowest point in our life, often referred to as the dark night of the soul. That's when every aspect of our life just seems to be enveloped in well... darkness! It's the moment when we throw up our hands and scream, either in our mind or in the room we are in at the time, "I just can't take this anymore!"

This is the moment we become open to help. The ego, that had been previously whispering in our inner ear, out of a habitual resistance to change saying, "I'm OK really" or "I can fix this myself" or "I can look after me fine thank you," dissolves for a few moments and we are forced to our spiritual knees. It's as if we are humbled into an openness to receiving help, into a surrender to whoever or whatever may assist us in our hour of greatest inner need. Very often this is the time when someone just happens to be present in our life who can point us towards a new, perhaps deeper, maybe more spiritual way of perceiving and thinking. If it's not a person, it may be a book that falls into our hands, or a leaflet or an invitation to some retreat that somewhat coincidentally arrives that very day!

The Journey Begins...or Does it?

These are significant moments that we may recognize, in retrospect, were turning points and the beginning of our spiritual journey. This book may be the first of many such points on your journey or just another of a growing collection. However, even though it seems we are waking up to deeper truths, those old habits still put up a fight. Having spent a lifetime developing the inclinations to feel sorry for ourselves, to be angry at others, to be fearful of the future or to be depressed about everything, they are just habits after all. Regardless of the techniques we try, despite the wisdom we may assimilate, no matter how many seminars we attend, at a deeper level those habits won't just disappear. It's as if many of them will fight to cling on, even though we may now clearly understand the what, why, when and how they are the source of the many forms of dis - ease we have been exploring here.

Why so Few Change!

Even though we fully realize intellectually that it's me and not other people that are making us suffer, the habit of believing our self to be the victim is hard to shift. It's like the reinforced steel and concrete foundation of an old and well established comfort zone that we would prefer not to demolish. Being a target is a familiar position. It's so much easier to be the victim. It's expected of us to be 'reactive' once someone has found the right buttons to press. So we prefer to live up to our victim reputation, indulge in our self perception as the presecuted one, rather than embark on a full-on internal engagement with the illusions that we ourselves are sustaining.

Why is it that, in reality, it seems so few people do change? Many talk a lot about change. They listen to and study the so-called 'experts of self change'. They enthusiastically attend the 'change your self' courses, seminars and workshops. They follow the trail to the promised pot of golden happiness at the end of the personal development and transformational rainbow! They go on long, often totally silent, retreats. They find a 'change coach' and get coached and mentored to... change! All with the aim of transforming themselves and thereby changing how they think, feel and live their life. Nothing wrong with any of that. The appropriate lessons are usually learned along the way according to our level of engagement. They may not be the expected lessons, the desired lessons. They may not deliver the AHA's promised on the promotional blurb. But something of value will happen during the course of any process that fosters self enquiry. Something will shift with the expansion of self awareness and an earnest engagement with one's own creative process.

However, it seems very few actually do change...deeply, significantly, permanently! Some even come out the other end of such self-empowerment and self-development events and processes with a piece of paper saying they are now a qualified 'transformational expert' with the credentials to teach others how to change! But their own behaviors, their reactions, their emotions, their personality, essentially stay the same. Why? It's those pesky habits! It's the attachment to the comfort of those uncomfortable comfort zones! It's the long and deep familiarity with their own unhappiness that they have grown to love...so to speak! Well, perhaps that's going a bit far!

Deep within our consciousness is a place, often called the subconscious, where we are attached to all these viral beliefs and it's not just a case of letting them go. After all, the vast majority are 'subconscious' attachments, which means they are outside our day-to-day, moment-to-moment awareness. And you can't let go of what you are not aware that you are holding on to! Mmm!

But then again, maybe you don't need to. Are you sitting uncomfortably? Then let's end with the only beginning!

A Revelation Revealed

One of the real secrets to change is that if you want to change you will need to stop trying to change!

There is an illusion that is often found at the heart of many of the schools of spiritual and personal development, at the heart of almost all personal growth and empowerment courses, workshops and seminars, at the core of most of tools, methods and techniques designed for 'self change'. It's the idea that YOU have to change, that YOU can change. But it's impossible. You cannot change your 'self'. What you can change is your creation, which is your personality, the matrix of habits, the inner scaffolding made up of all your previously developed traits and tendencies. They are your unique constructions. But 'they' are not you - they are your creation. Your personality, is not the 'I' that says, "I am." Your personality is not you!

The I, the self, the conscious aware being that you and I are, never changes. We only 'believe' that we do. But we don't. However, because you identify your self with your physical form. Because you identify with your personality, with the matrix of habits and tendencies that you have created, even with the emotions that you feel, all of which do change, you fall under the illusion that it's you who is changing, can change, needs to change, will have to change!

This insight, this realization of the deepest 'truth' about you, and me, and everyone, truly is a game changer...so to speak!

Enlightenment Beckons

In Part Two we explored many of the truths that, when fully realized, have the power to dispel the beliefs that cause the many dis - eases of consciousness. 'Realized truth' heals consciousness of the dis - eases caused by those 'viral beliefs'. The deepest truth which has the power to eliminate all dis

- eases of the soul is the simple truth about who and what you are. Simply because all those dis - eases (you may have noticed) have a common cause, namely you attaching to, and identifying with, what you are not!

We lose awareness of this truth of who we are when we become distracted by the world, attracted to the world, attached to something or someone in the world and finally addicted to the stimulations of worldly experiences. It's not right or wrong, it just 'happens'. The truth of who you are is not a 'truth' as in an intellectual observation or reflection, but truth as in your 'true state of being'.

In other words, we lose our awareness of, and the ability to live from, our true state of being. This happens the moment we become attached to, and identify with, material forms in the world out there and mental forms in the world of our consciousness 'in here'. That all starts with the mistaken belief that we are the image that we see reflected back to us from any mirror. This mistake then expands to identifying with the manufacturer's label of whatever our form is wearing in the mirror! Which will expand to include ideas based on what we drive, where we work and who we have partnered! All these attachments generate a stream of separate identities in our own mind. Eventually our deepest and most subtle attachments/identities will be to those invisible and intangible 'viral beliefs' that we assimilate from the world around us on our journey through life.

Gradually, these learned beliefs become subtly woven through our consciousness as they diminish and distort our true state of being. It's a state in which there is a natural, clear awareness of 'who I am'. These beliefs could be likened to the 'impurities' found in metals as they are mined. Before the purity of the metal can be restored the impurities need to be extracted. It's as if these beliefs are imputities that 'endarken' our consciosness. Hence the great prize of 'enlightenment' that is often positioned as the reward of spiritual practice and perhaps years of focussed spiritual effort.

When there is a moment of 'enlightenment' there is a brief restoration of 'absolute clarity'. This is a moment when we are released from the grip of all these beliefs. All the separate, false identities are demolished. The awareness of our true state is restored. Not as something that is known. More a silent state of thoughtless knowingness! But it tends only to be for a moment. Then we realise how deeply ingrained within our consciousness these illusions about our self really are. They keep 'popping' back into our consciousness like interfering neighbours. It's those habits again.

So while we can keep refreshing that realization of 'who I am', usually through meditative practice, it seems we can only regain and maintain that 'true self awareness' by also seeing and realizing who we are NOT. It's only when we start to examine and 'strip off', ALL the beliefs we have assimilated that we can see and fully realize, that a) I am not my beliefs, b) I am not the form that I 'believe' I am, in other words you are not who or what you have been taught to believe you are, c) the beliefs that I am holding on to are not the truth.

One Essential Insight into Essence

Many words are used to describe the energy of consciousness that we each are. Soul, spirit, the authentic self, the unconditioned self, are all appropriate. I've used most of them somewhere here including the 'I' that says, "I am." These are ways to 'point at' what the 'I' is! Because words can only 'point'.

All of that can be roughly translated into one essenceful insight, *you are 'no one' and I am 'no one' and we are all 'no one'!*

This is not an easy idea to get one's head around. But that's the thing, don't try. Don't try to make it an idea and then just another story about 'me'. That's what we do with the name given to our physical form. It becomes an idea, a belief that your name and form are what you are, and then you create a story made up of more beliefs and lots of memories built around your name and form. But that name and form and the stories are not what you are. You are not a name or form. And you are not a story. These are 'created' images and ideas and you are the creator, you are not an image or an idea.

Being No One again!
Look at it this way. When you believe you are your name/form then, when someone insults your name/form, you will be upset, which equals a moment of dis - ease. If you believe you are what you do then, when someone criticizes what you do, you will be sad or angry, probably both, which equals dis - ease. If you believe you are your religion then, when someone ridicules your religious beliefs, you will take it personally and argue, which equals friction and maybe anger, which equals dis - ease. All the dis - eases of the soul have their origin in a misplaced sense of who and what I AM! That's why our biggest, deepest and most frequent habit by far, is misplacing our sense of who and what we are. To many, especially those who have already stepped onto a 'spiritual path', all this may sound elementary. However the subtle layers of illusion about our self reach deep down into our consciousness. Whenever you 'react' emotionally to anything or anyone you know there is still another layer, another habit of attachment and misidentifcation to be disolved!

It's only when you start 'noticing' and thereby discovering these subtle layers for your self, within your self, that the deepest part of the journey from awareness to realization to transformation can begin. Where transformation doesn't mean change but the transcending of the subtle 'mental forms' you have been mistakenly identifying your self with.

No one and no thing is what the being that you are is!

Gratitude and Humility

When you restore that awareness, you will also realize that you have 'always' been no one and no thing. And you realize that 'no one' and 'no thing' cannot be changed! You cannot change that primary, some say eternal, core state of being. All you can do is restore your awareness that 'ultimately' and forever you are no one and no thing. As you do, nothing changes outwardly. You still eat, sleep, work, play, pay the bills etc. But as you reawaken that awareness, you no longer need to create and sustain an image in the eyes of others. Because you now know any image upon which you base your sense of self is an illusion.

You no longer need to be attached to anything or anyone. So you don't need to think about 'how do I detach and be non-dependent', it just occurs naturally. You no longer need anything from others or from the world to bolster any illusion you 'used' to have about where you thought you 'had to go' and what you believed you 'had to do' in order to be successful, happy and fulfilled. Success is realizing you are already content and you are already filled full of all that is necessary to live a full and happy life. All those old habits of 'wanting' and 'attaching' fall away naturally. Everything that you think and do then comes from a place of gratitude and humility. Everything that you see happening 'out there' is perceived to be what is 'meant' to be. You can now see, from an inner space of understanding and acceptance, that all is well and all will be well.

The Game of Life

Now that's not to say that when you go through passport control and show your passport you say, "Well that's not really me, I am no one really!" It doesn't mean you don't show up for work and stop playing the role of whatever position you have or doing whatever job you do. It doesn't mean you hand out blank business cards with no one and no thing on it and say, "Well this is me and this is what I do...nothing!" It doesn't mean you don't have discussions about the deeper meaning of the scriptural texts that interest your intellect.

We live in a world of embodied souls, a world where we get to play with and through a physical form. The language that we all co-create and share in that process is essentially the 'language of labels'. Keep speaking the language and keep playing the game of life, the creative game of living. But experiment with eliminating what many now see as the most common mistake we all make, which is 'identifying' with the labels. Try 'not believing' the label is what you are. Can you see, in your conversation, moments of labelling? When you become aware of a 'labelling moment' you will start to notice that it's the labeling that takes all the fun and lightness out of the game of life. It ushers in many moments of dis - ease.

Deep down, we know in our heart that life really is just a game. A playful game that is intended to be an experience of delight and joy, of wonder and laughter. But the moment we forget that is the same moment we forget to be no one and no thing. The moment we believe and try to be someone and something, that's when the dis - ease called 'seriousness' kicks in and joy disappears.

Create and Play

So when you do, truly, authentically realize that you are, in essence, no-one and no thing, then everything else is seen to be what it is. A game, a play, a workshop, a journey, a meeting...you decide, because you have restored your power to create the world and your life in the world, in whatever way you choose. But no longer do you, can you, take what you see 'out there' in the world to be the one and only reality. You no longer see it as the primary reality, as you previously believed it was. It is a very secondary reality and as a creator you will see both the world, and your journey through life in the world, is just the context in which you get to be creative, to play, to be loving, to be loved and to be joyful...in the company of friends. Everyone becomes your friend.

The moment you start to take anything seriously, notice the presence of fear, the most popular dis - ease of the soul. That's the signal that you have just fallen asleep, again, to who you are. You have lost awareness of the real you. You have just started believing, again, that you are just what you see in that mirror, that you are what you do, that you are where you live etc. The consequent illusion of mortality will then kick in and that will make you perceive the world 'out there' as a dangerous place. Dis - ease again!

Awakening from your Dream

In the process of realizing or restoring your awareness of who you really are, which is no-one and no thing, there will be an oscillation between awakeness and sleepiness, between moments of being fully aware and moments when you lose the clarity of that awareness.

When you are awake and aware, you know you do not need to change, that YOU cannot change. You 'know' it's both unnecessary and ultimately impossible for YOU to change. And you know that there is no point in trying to change the world around you because, in your awakened state, you have also realized that everything out there in the world is appearing and moving and changing exactly as it should. It's not your job to police the universe! With those two realizations, you are at peace with your self and at peace with the world.

Waking up spiritually can be likened to awakening from a deep physical sleep. When we sleep in our beds, we dream. On awakening in the morning, we realize what we dreamt was just that, a dream. Therefore not real. One sign that we are waking up to who/what we really are is when we start to notice our day-to-day life has become more 'dreamlike'. We will start to notice how we interpret the world, and events in the world, according to how we see our self, according to who and what we 'believe' we are and according to the beliefs we have inherited and assimilated from others about the world itself.

For example, when you identify your self with what you do then, when you hear on the news that cuts are being made in your industry, you create a mental story which includes an imagined loss of job, so fear arises. This means that, although you think you are awake, and you are physically, although everything looks and feels real, you are in a dream-like state of consciousness. Your fearfulness is arising out of an identity that is based on what you do. But that sense of identity is an illusion, it's like a dream, a fiction, that you are creating about your self within your consciousness. When you consider your self to be such a 'fictional character', then all your interpretations of the world are filtered through the 'fictional you'. Those interpretations then become fiction themselves! Starting to be aware of that is one of the main signs you are 'waking up'.

Rediscovering Reality!

As we have seen the 'reality' is you are not what you do. You are just you, the conscious aware being. You are just the 'I' that says, "I am." From that state of consciousness, you watch the secondary reality of the world out there changing color, texture and form. And in this case the change is happening to something called 'an industry' and a workplace. Because you no longer identify your self with what you do, you do not create a story of future loss, you do not create fear, you do not suffer, you do not live in a self-created mental dream! You are free, you are awake, you are aware. The world changes, you don't, jobs change, you don't, everything comes and goes, you don't. You always remain. You are the primary reality in your own life.

If we are deluded about who and what we are, so we will create delusional and illusory interpretations about what's happening 'out there' in the world. Our version of reality out there is distorted according to our illusory sense of self. But so entrenched in our consciousness are all our illusory identities such as ("I am my form, I am what I do, I am my nationality," etc.) that we don't realize we are interpreting and distorting the world out there according to our false sense of who/what we are 'in here'.

Living in a Dream

If, for example, we have learned to believe that only high achievers are successful and happy people in the world, we start to rush around our life attempting to be a great achiever. We start hunting for success in the eyes of others so that we can be happy. It will probably take a great big brick wall with stress written all over it to bring us to our senses with the eventual realization that success is relative and our happiness is not dependent on any external achievement. But we lived in a dreamlike state when we were seeing our self as a 'great future achiever' chasing... achievement!

This is why that old cliché 'I am living the dream' really means living in a state of unreality! One day, I realized that I don't want or need to 'live the dream', I need to awaken 'from the dream' that I am already creating and living! Only then is it possible to be contented, which is the deepest form of happiness. Only then is it possible to be joyful, which is the happiness that comes from inside out when you have realized you don't 'want' anything from anyone, when you realize you did not come to 'get a life', you came to create your life! Being creative is the true purpose and function of consciousness. It's only when we are true to our nature that we can be creative in a way that is aligned to our true and real self. Only then can we know true joy.

All these moments of dis - ease that we 'insperience' within our consciousness are primary 'signals' that we are both generating and participating in our own self-made dream. We have absorbed the beliefs of others into our consciousness and in so doing sabotaged our own creativity. When everyone holds the same beliefs, they dream almost the same illusions and delusions, and the result is the confusion, chaos and craziness that we see so often in the world around us today. And yet, in another sense, a truer sense, a deeper sense, the world is not crazy and chaotic, as whatever is happening is exactly what is meant to be happening! We don't call the decay and destruction of autumn crazy or chaotic, it's just another season arriving at the appropriate time!

Our attachment to our 'viral beliefs' ensures that we don't notice our own misinterpretations. We don't notice that we are, in essence, dreaming the world. And when someone challenges our beliefs, it becomes our cue to trigger the belief that it's always the other person's beliefs and interpretations that are delusional. Until one day, we start to notice and feel something is not quite right, something doesn't add up, something is missing, something is disturbing me and it's not something out there in the world. It's in me! That subtle feeling, that quiet intuition or that brick wall moment, is one of the first signs of a self/soul re-awakening to itself. It is the soul awakening to the realization that it is nothing more than consciousness itself, and not the form or the many labels for the form, that we all learn to blindly 'believe' we are.

At first, each day will be filled with moments which alternate between waking and sleeping, between awareness and unawareness, until you fully realize the origin and nature of all the illusions that you have been creating to make up your dream about...you!

There are four practices that, when built into your life, ensure that you will gradually awaken fully from your sleepiness and replace the dream, that you didn't realize you were subconsciously creating, with reality. They are not practices that require occasional attention. They require daily attention. These are the four practices that ensure the immune system of the soul regains and maintains it's ability to access the truths required to encircle and extinguish the viral beliefs that are cause of both the dreams and the dis - eases that occur within our consciousness.

The First Practice - MEDITATION

"Don't just sit there, do something" is the mantra of a world addicted to action and reaction. A world that is run by the belief that when things are not going smoothly, 'something has to be done and quickly!' Have you ever noticed that seldom does that kind of 'reactiveness' make the world a better, more loving, more harmonious place. "Don't just do something, sit there" is the wisdom of an enlightened soul who has realized their peace, their power and their wisdom come from inside out. They have learned that action informed by a patient wisdom is usually more effective than a reaction informed by an emotional disturbance?

In many ways, life only begins when we realize that our inner peace and our inner power are 'already present' states of being. They are not states to be achieved through going somewhere, doing something or finding someone. Up until that point, we search for peace and power outside our self. The 'don't just do something, sit there' approach does not mean we always sit around doing nothing and that life is one long sitting! Action that is imbued with peace and shaped by the power of our wisdom is action that extends love to others and not further (emotional) dis - ease within our self.

Meditation is one way to reconnect with that underlying peaceful and powerful state of being. It is one way to restore the 'true vibration' of the energy of consciousness. Meditation is one way 'to know' our self as we are, as powerful entities, as loving beings, as joyful individuals, as intrinsically peaceful but proactive entities. As we have seen, we lose that ability to be and know our true self as soon as we are taught to lose our sense of identity in anything we are not!

Every day, the world around you wants you to identify with what you are not! It's called marketing and advertising, entertainment and politics. It's the job of these worlds to keep you asleep in a dreamlike state, to keep you asleep to who you are by convincing you to identify with what 'they are', with what 'they have', with what 'they do' and with what 'they believe'. However, even they know not what they do, as they are asleep themselves!

'Practice' is probably not the best words to describe meditation. 'Art' is probably better. Ultimately meditation is not something that you do, it is the art of restoring your true 'state of being' i.e. being your true self, wherever you are and during whatever you are doing. Most of us will spend our entire life trying to be somebody. Because that's what most of us are taught to believe we have to do to 'get on'. So it's easy to get caught up by the belief that we 'have to make something of ourselves'. That belief makes us watch other people to see how they are doing, to measure and aspire to their success and then to wonder why our life doesn't seem to be so fulfilled. It's a mental rollercoaster that essentially goes nowhere.

Perfection and Beauty

There is an old saying which restores a truth to our awareness which, when fully realized, will help us step off that particular rollercoaster. *Those who are trying to 'be somebody' don't yet know how 'to be'.* It's only when we STOP trying to be something, someone, some kind of 'human doing' who is capable of attracting the attention and validation of others, that we can finally BE our self. When we are being our self we notice that ALL that we were previously seeking through trying to be someone is already there. The 'ALL' that's already there means there is within us all a peace that surpasseth all other pleasure, there is a contentment that surpasseth all other excitements, there is a serenity that surpasseth all others tranquilities, there is a love that surpasseth all other affections. All are already there within our being!

Being in that state of being consequently changes our priorities, our purpose and our personal way of relating to others. However it's best not to speak of it, only to live it until it's more fully restored and you are relatively stable in such a liberated state. Between here and there will be moments of oscillation between sleepiness and awakeness, between awareness of the ALL and unawareness of it all...so to speak! It takes time to restore the perfection and beauty of virtue to our character. It takes a little time to fully awaken our awareness of being no one and no thing. It takes a little time to restore to our awareness the peace, the power and the love that we can only 'know' once we have realised we are no one!

The art and practice of meditation is the cultivation of self **awareness**, the invocation of **realization** then the subsequent **transformation**. Not just the transformation of one's 'self', as the self restores the awareness of it's original form. But the forms of all that one is creating, from thoughts to attitudes, from perceptions to behaviors, from beliefs to emotions. As the old saying goes, "Infinite patience creates instant results!" Meditation is the instant patience with infinite results.

The Artful Practice of Meditation
Meditation is essentially the art of being! It starts with quiet moments, in a quiet corner somewhere, quietly sitting and being, just being, quiet! Then noticing the habits of doing that want to take over, noticing the thoughts and feelings that want to jump up and out and into action. Then gently saying to all of them, "No, not just now, be still and know I am peace." When you are at peace you will know that peace

is what you are. No longer is it an idea or an aspiration or a promise, it is what 'I am'.

We live in the world of action. We live in bodies. We interact with others and with the natural energies of the world around us. If we are to free our self from our habits of attachment and misidentification, from our habits of wanting and aspiring to be somebody other than what we are, it helps to realise that while we are in the world we are not of the world. We are simply passing through.

In meditation, you will 'see through' all the illusory beliefs and images you have assimilated and created 'about' your self. You will strip off all the ideas and images, memories and concepts that you have used to build your sense of identity, until there is just the awareness of the 'I' that says, "I am." Anything after 'I am' is not you. It's a fiction, a construct, a figment of your imagination! Whatever you say after 'I am' is not what you are. Even to say, "I am consciousness" or "I am a soul" is not true, because they are words that bring forth concepts. And you/I/we are not concepts. We are the creators of concepts. The painter is not the painting!

So when you sit to meditate, have no aim, no expectation, no desire for any particular insperience. Sit 'in' your body, sit on the throne of your awareness and just watch. See how everything comes and goes - thoughts, feelings, memories, impressions - all come and go, rise and fall. But notice who is watching. Who is it that never comes and goes? You. The I. Yes there is a 'you', there is an 'I', a sense of 'I'ness. And it's OK. Don't try to grasp it. Don't look for it. Don't 'expect' to feel anything. Not so easy after a lifetime of habitual looking, grasping and expecting.

The moment will come. It will occur. You will see. You will know. You will be. Just be.

Ultimately, there is no single 'right way' to meditate. So if that's all a bit vague or a bit too esoteric for your taste, take ten minutes and try this way.

Sit in a quiet space where you won't be disturbed. Let your body take the shape of the chair. Consciously relax your body in the chair. Scan your body with your awareness for any places of tightness or tension. Allow relaxation to happen in those places. Now let your attention follow your breath. Just for a few moments. Gently concentrate on your breathing. Don't separate the 'in breath' from the 'out breath'. Watch it as one complete movement. As you do, you will notice you become even more relaxed. Then bring your attention to your self. Be aware of your self being...aware. Then create one thought within your awareness, "I am a being of peace." Allow that one thought to receive the energy of your attention. Like watering a flower, let that thought grow by giving it the water of your gentle attention. Turn up the brightness of that thought. If you are distracted or your attention strays, come back and start again. Then, after a few moments, let the thought dissolve. Let it gently fade into the background. Notice what remains. A 'feeling' of peace. There is just a feeling of deep peace. The mind is quiet. There is a stillness here at the heart of your being. You are silent and still. Silent and still. Silent ..... and .....still. Be in that stillness. Listen to the silence. Then bring your awareness back to your body, to the chair, to the room around you. Come back into the here and now of the room around you. But bring that stillness with you. As you look through your eyes, look from that stillness. As you listen with your ears, listen from that stillness. As you talk, speak from that stillness. Then notice how your stillness enters the room and how those around you become a little more still, a little more peaceful, in themselves. For a few moments at least.

The Second Practice - CONTEMPLATION

Meditation is not enough to awaken fully to being who you are which is no one and no thing. It's not enough to ensure that you stay awake and aware consistently in all situations and circumstances. It has to be combined with three other practices; contemplation, application and contribution. Contemplation means occasionally staring into infinity while you do one of two things:

Reflect on an Experience Just Passed.

For example, you just got upset with someone. But what exactly was the emotion? Name the dis - ease you felt! Why did you suffer? Can you see that it was what YOU thought or did that made YOU upset, not them? Why? What, within you, caused you to react? Is there a pattern? Was there something that you wanted or you believed you were not getting? Who were you trying to be when you reacted? Can you see that your moment of dis - ease arose becasue you were trying to be someone that you are not?

Be gentle with your reflective and contemplative self enquiry. Be curiously fascinated but not obsessively investigative.

Read and Reflect on the Wisdom of Another

Choose some small nugget of another's wisdom and 'mine' it for meaning and insight within your own consciousness. Is what they say true for you? If not, why not? Is there a reason why you resonate so strongly with what they say? Is there a reason why you resist what they indicate? What else does this wisdom reveal? Where does it lead you next?

Internal contemplation is the spiritual equivalent of academic study in the world. But it's far from academic.

It produces moments when you see and realize a deeper meaning of what you thought you knew, a deeper insight into what you previously took at face value, AHA! moments arise, realization occurs. Contemplation helps you to reinterpret the world and your experience of the world with greater accuracy and, in so doing, it will reveal exactly how you create the world...within you!

In contemplation, you are reviewing, reflecting and thinking, whereas in meditation, you are going beyond the limitations of memory and thought. In contemplation, you are exploring the connections between insights, generating new meaning. In meditation, you are not looking for anything, not wanting anything. In meditation you access your inner power. In contemplation, you are accessing your inner wisdom. Power and wisdom are your own priceless personal inner resources. But only you can access them for your self. This is why spirituality, or 'waking up' to the truth that spirit is what you are, can never be an academic subject

Remember you are not trying to change you. You are waking up to who you are and have been all along. The practices of meditation and contemplation will awaken you from your dream as they help you to 'cast off' all your illusions. If you want to!

The Third Practice - APPLICATION

While there tends to be patterns in the way we live that make each day seem similar to yesterday, in reality every day is different. Every moment is unique, never to be repeated. Every action and interaction is different. That's why every day and every interaction is an opportunity to apply what you are realizing. As you awaken your awareness to deeper truths through meditation and contemplation, you are invoking and evoking realization. You start to clearly see what is true as opposed to what is false. If you don't act on what you are realizing and rediscovering within your self, you miss the opportunity to bridge the gap between theory and practice, between the ideal and the real, between dreaming life and being fully awake in life.

The old tendencies and traits, all those old habits of your personality, only fall away completely when there is new action, shaped by your personal realizations of what is true. They lose their hold over YOU. Like a set of padlocked chains surrounding your body, the padlock called 'belief' springs open, and the chains of all the illusions that arise from all those 'viral beliefs' fall freely away. With that freedom comes a peace and contentment that is as natural as the color yellow is for a daffodil. But it only happens when you act on what you realize, only when you consciously allow the realization of your trueness to inform and shape your attitudes and behaviors.

Every day provides countless opportunities to be your natural, awakened self; to bring your true nature, which is peaceful, loving and joyful, into your exchanges with others. Then you will also to notice why, in some moments and in some situations, you aren't yet able to do that.

Remember, you are not applying and practicing in order to change your 'self', but in order to 'reveal and restore' your unchanging stable state of being, which WAS and IS always there! Sometimes you just have to be aware of what's in the way simply because, in such moments, what's IN the way IS the way!

Three questions for reflection on the application of your realizations:

1 What does the day ahead look like?

2 List the specific situations in which you could apply what you have realized.

3 Assign one realization to each situation.

The Fourth Practice - CONTRIBUTION

The moment we are born into this world, the vast majority of us are born into one particular 'viral belief system'. It is a belief system that is responsible for the destruction of untold lives, not to mention the daily shattering of human happiness for billions of people. It is a system that says 'in order to live a happy life you must desire and acquire, accumulate and possess'. No-one seems able to explain that to follow this 'viral edict', that is built into the culture of almost every society, is to act against the grain of life itself. It is to defy nature, both the nature of the self and the nature of the world.

It's our nature to give, to radiate our energy, outwards into the world of our relationships with others and into the world itself. It is not our nature to try to bring the world to us. Yet most of us develop and live with the tendency to attempt to get something from the world, acquire something from someone in the world, believing it's the way life works. We don't notice that this viral belief and intention is at the root of most of our daily stress and suffering. It's what is literally making us unhappy. It is both the symptom and the cause of all our moments of dis - ease in all our relationships. Yes, a moment of acquisition does give us a buzz, it gives us a lift, a boost that some would call happiness. But it's not real happiness, it's just stimulation, which is why it doesn't last and why we also develop within our personality the habit of 'thirsting for more'. Regardless of what we believe we have acquired, we still want more.

So it's highly recommended that you find a context in your life where you just give. Wanting absolutely nothing in return. What you give can be at any level - time, energy, help, advice, support. It's the intention that is key here. It's the line from intention to action that requires the motivation 'to give' free of all expectation for anything in return. The consequent satisfaction that comes from within is the sign that the habit of wanting and taking is losing its power to govern your behavior and therefore losing its power to make you miserable! All you need do is check if you have any hidden agenda behind your altruistic contribution. It's a subtle agenda. Watch out for any kind of expectation as it's the first symptom of inevitable dis - ease!

You will quickly start to notice three things. First, there is a feeling that comes from deep within. It is the feeling of your 'giving power'. It will eventually be accompanied by a clear awareness of your immense value. Second, there grows a greater and deeper appreciation and understanding of what others are experiencing as you naturally empathize (not sympathize) with those to whom you are extending your self. Third, the old habits of gimme gimme gimme, the old threads of wanting and desiring, that previously held the cloak of your personality together, start to atrophy and lose their hold over your motives and intentions. Unhappiness is on its way out the door, for all unhappiness is essentially derived from the 'belief' that I am not getting what 'I want'!

Four a Day! Plus One

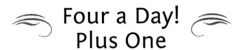

It's the combination of all four practices above that serve to facilitate and sustain your awakening and the healing of all the dis - eases of the soul that we have explored in this book, and more!

If you want to speed up the whole process there is a fifth practice. Hang out with people who are also practicing with the intention of awakening. Being in the 'energy field' of people with the same spiritual intention and focus, same motivation and interest, is like those little particles they send around the tunnels of CERN in Switzerland. It's the presence of a powerful electromagnetic field that makes them move faster. Similarly, it is the 'spiritual energy field' of a community of people who are waking up together that both deepens and accelerate our personal process. Not that we are in a hurry, of course.

The particles at CERN are also guided to deliberately smash together so that scientists can observe the resulting behavior. In a spiritual community, there is no intention to deliberately smash into each other but there will be inevitable moments when personalities start rubbing together, grating on each other and yes the occasional 'smashing' together. Not through any physical violence, just through encountering each other and being mirrors for each other. These are priceless moments, because they give us the opportunity to watch and observe, to examine and understand our own behavior, our own reactions. Only then can we get a sense of how awake and aware we are. Only in such moments can we get some measure of our progress as we reinvigorate and restore the immune system of the soul to full working order!

Only then do we know how well we are in our being.

Coach Your Self to Wellness

The past decade has seen the rise and rise of coaching. Partly out of the recognition that we can help each other to awaken to our full potential. Partly because an increasing number of people are looking to change the trajectory of their life and create a career path that is of greater service to others. Coaching has become an 'in thing' to aspire to and to do.

But like counseling, it is not a skill or an art that can be mastered in a weekend seminar or even over the course of a series of formal workshops. It is only truly developed in parallel with a deliberately cultivated awareness of what is happening within oneself, as well as frequent engagement with others in conversations about deep spiritual things!

So here is your opportunity to practice on your self with a little bit of self-coaching. This would fall fully into the second practice of CONTEMPLATION. One of the key skills of a great coach is the ability to ask the right question in order to allow the coachee to find their own answers, to generate their own 'realizations'. The following exercise is about happiness. All the dis - eases that we've been exploring here are also symptoms of a loss of personal happiness. The cause, as we have seen, is always a set of viral beliefs that we have assimilated and empowered to shape our feelings, thoughts and actions.

When it comes to happiness, the beliefs that 'interfere' are not only viral, they are 'toxic' to our consciousness. So here, in this the final part of our time together, are a few reflections on authentic happiness and some of the most toxic beliefs that 'kill it'. There are questions for your own personal contemplation and reflection. Questions that, if you use them effectively, should lead you to remember, realize and reveal the truths that you already know deep within your self.

If you did not already know what is true, you would become like a crazy person with no sense of how to think, relate and live in this world. You would have almost no intelligence whatsoever. Truth is the only cure for the viral and toxic beliefs that cause all our dis - eases and ultimately all our bodies diseases. It only needs to be realized and brought back to life and you will be a well being again.

Detoxing Consciousness to Restore Authentic Happiness

If someone said you are forever happy even when you are having feelings of despair, depression and you are, as they say, 'down in the dumps', would you believe them? If someone said happiness was your real, true, underlying, original and eternal nature despite your prevailing mawkish moods or the reality of those 'Monday morning miseries', would you believe them? If someone told you the holy grail of happiness has been residing within your heart all along, despite the world convincing you that you can only find it in a department store, would you believe them?

Almost everything we do and pursue is motivated by the search for happiness. Yet it seems no one has been able to explain to us what happiness is exactly or how to experience it precisely. As a consequence, it's been confused with many other feelings, clouded by many false promises and lost in the mists of many illusions.

Happiness is a state of being. But it's hard to pin down an accurate description of happiness as it's a state that you 'feel' and the words that we use for different feelings mean different things to different people. But here goes anyway. See if this 'feels right' to you!

If you sit and reflect on 'what is happiness', for a few moments at least, it's likely you will come up with three predominant feelings when you are authentically happy - **contentment, joy** and **bliss**. Not contentment as in a kind of soporific laziness, not joy as in an excited scream when the new baby arrives, not bliss as in a substance-induced state or when your team wins! So what kind of contentment, joy and bliss?

Authentic happiness includes a CONTENTMENT which occurs naturally when nothing and no one can disturb you. You no longer have any buttons that can be pressed! It's a contentment that's only possible when you no longer 'desire' anything or anyone simply because you've realized you no longer 'need' anything or anyone else to 'make you'... happy! As long as there is desire there will always be some discontentment!

Contentment occurs in those moments when you are able to accept everyone as they are and everything as it is, at all times, in all places, at all moments! Remember, acceptance does not mean you agree with others or that you condone what others have done. It's a serene acceptance born of the recognition that, in the words of Desiderata *everything is unfolding exactly as it should.* It sounds easy but it's not, simply because the work we will need to do includes not attaching to any ideas of how we want the world and other people to be, and not identifying with any thing or anyone in the world! No small inner challenge!

Authentic happiness includes a JOY that arises naturally from deep within when you are engaged in the process of what you/I/we are designed to do, which is to 'be creative'. Not creative as in painting and poetry, or even making something in the world. But the deepest form of creativity, which is bringing your true nature, your true state, which is peaceful and loving, into the world through different forms, including the forms of your intentions, the forms of your thoughts, the forms of your attitudes and the forms of your behaviors. These are the primary forms that we all create. They are the forms of life and living that each one of us gets the opportunity to create simply by being alive. However, recognition of this level of creativity only takes place when we realize we ourselves are not a 'physical form' but the energy of consciousness, the energy of the formless being sometimes called soul. This is the spiritual energy that 'we are' as we animate and 'come through' the physical form that we occupy. Joy starts to arise again from within when there is the realization that I didn't come to get a life, I came to create a life, with others.

Authentic happiness includes a BLISS that arises naturally as long as we remain internally free. Watch and listen to the young sallows on a warm summers evening as they learn to fly. Listen to them scream in ecstacy as they zig zag across the sky. They are 'delighting' in the freedom of flight. It's a great metaphor for spirit, for our life. We do taste the delight and the bliss of this kind of freedom but only very occasionally. Why? Because most of the time we are not internally free. Why? Because we learn to become attached and therefore fearful of losing the objects of our attachment. It's attachment that keeps us anchored and yet insecure. We sabotage our own inner freedom with any form of attachment. Where there is attachment there is fear and where there is fear there cannot be the bliss of authentic happiness.

The Natural State of Happiness

There is an idea, some call it an insight, others call it obvious, that says consciousness (the self) starts out like water - pure and natural, free of all toxins or any form of pollution. It's only over time, after water arrives on the earth from the clouds up above, that it starts to absorb and be polluted by a variety of toxins. As a result, it loses its purity, its naturalness. Its original state is compromised. We are now very aware of all the toxins that our water contains. Many people spend much money on water purification systems so that their physical health will not be compromised. They try to extract the seven toxins which, by many accounts, are now found in our tap water - fluoride, chlorine, radioactive substances, pharmaceuticals, chromium, heavy metals and arsenic - but there are probably more!

Could it be a similar process with what we call happiness? Could happiness be an original, pure and natural state of... consciousness? Could it be that our consciousness has been polluted and compromised by a variety of toxins? Each one of us cannot know the answer to these questions until we check into the laboratory of our consciousness, our self, make our own investigations and see for ourselves. Articles and books, seminars and retreats may 'help us', meditation and contemplation practices may assist us to look in the right direction, to recognize whether it's true or not. But it's only when we can 'see' and 'realize' for our self what is sabotaging our 'natural happiness', our pure happy state, that we can clean out the toxins and set our self free.

One the primary aims of effective coaching is to help the coachee to ask themselves the right questions so they may enhance their self awareness and cultivate the 'insightful realizations' of what is getting in the way of their happiness. So let's test the 'happiness is natural' theory and see if we can find the right questions which, when used self reflectively, may help us to recognize the toxins within our consciousness that are polluting and poisoning our natural state of happiness.

While the water that comes out of our tap 'seems' to be pure, we are, at the same time, aware that it's not. Similarly with our state of happiness. What 'seems' to be feelings of happiness usually aren't our true and natural state of happiness. Some of the signs that the happiness that we believe we are feeling is not 'authentic' is that our feelings are usually dependent on something or someone 'out there'. There is no consistency, as what we believe is a feeling of happiness comes and goes. It rises and falls in intensity. It is not an energizing feeling, but over time, it is draining.

If you watch out for these symptoms it means something toxic has polluted your consciousness. These toxins are another set of learned beliefs. It seems there is a variety of 'toxic beliefs' that underlie the habit of creating 'false happiness'. Here are seven of the main toxic beliefs that have established themselves within our consciousness. These are popular toxins that we all tend to have absorbed, mostly when we were young. See if you recognize them within your self.

Toxic Belief No 1
Acquisition Makes me Happy!

We believe that if we acquire certain objects, certain 'partners', then we will find happiness. However most people who have acquired more than they need will usually confirm that acquisition only brings a temporary stimulation at best and a false sense of security at worst. It also brings an increased responsibility in the form of more things to think about, which for many means 'worry about'! And if we are not careful, we easily use our acquisitions to create a false self image as we try to impress others. We confuse our wealth with our worth! However it can be an addictive way to try to be happy because there is always that initial thrill of a new acquisition. But it always wears off. So the toxic belief that acquisition brings happiness requires elimination, otherwise we may just become addicted to accumulation!

The coaching questions for self-reflection: What do you want that you 'believe' will make you happy? Make a list. Then ask your self if you are sure these things will bring authentic happiness. If not, why not?

Toxic Belief Number 2
Achievement Makes me Happy

This is the belief that has us continuously setting goals, then using our time and energy in striving and struggling towards their achievement. No bad thing, some would say. It is important to have a focus for your energy, others would say. However, when we believe achievement brings happiness and we focus time and energy on achieving, we tend to do two things that will ensure our unhappiness. We tend to delay our happiness until the goal is achieved. We will likely create a partiular fear along the way known as the worry that we may not make it. Sometimes a more subtle belief kicks in. It says you have to 'deserve' to be happy. That means you have to work hard to be happy, you have to earn your happiness. This is often referred to as the Scottish Protestant work ethic! An almost cast iron guarantee of perpetual unhappiness!

 The coaching questions for self-reflection: What are you aiming to achieve that you believe will make you happy? Make a list. Then ask your self, are you sure these achievements will make you happy? If not why not?

Toxic Belief No 3
Excitement equals Happiness

This belief tends to be learned when we are very young. Parents simply pass on the illusion that excitement is happiness when they take us to our first circus or sporting occassion. They become excited and call it happiness so we believe them. They know not what they teach! Excitement is what happens when the water in the kettle boils. The molecules are excited, they are agitated. But happiness for a human being is not agitation. Happiness is, as we saw earlier, a state of contentment with a natural flow of joy from our heart into the world.

 The coaching questions for self-reflection: What do you use to excite yourself believing that it makes you happy? Make a list. Then ask your self, are you sure these excitements are real happiness? If not why not?

Toxic Belief No 4
Happiness is Dependent on Others

We all know the moment when we have said, "I was so happy when you said that! You made me so happy." But did they? Does someone else make you happy? It seems that way. And that's what most of us have been taught. We forget that we are ourselves responsible for our own state of being, therefore our state of happiness. When we make our feelings dependent on what other people say and on their behavior towards us, it's probably one of the hardest toxins to eliminate from our consciousness. One question can start the process of self liberation, "Who exactly is responsible for my personal happiness?" Can you be contented no matter what anyone says or does? If not, why not? What is it within us that is so reliant on what others say and do? Perhaps another useful question for reflection is; what 'seems' to be missing within us? What is clouding our awareness of our natural contentment?

More coaching questions for self-reflection: Who are you dependent upon in your life to make you happy? Make a list. Then ask your self if they really do make you happy. Are they really responsible for your happiness? If not why not?

Toxic Belief No 5
Happiness is the Result of Attachment

"That's mine, they are mine, this is my house, my car, my money, my partner, my children". These are usually moments when we are really saying we need to be attached to these things in order to be happy. How do we know that all 'mineness', all attachment, will only bring unhappiness? Because there will be frequent moments of anxiety, tension, worry and even panic as we 'fear' losing what we are attached to. Each of those moments are unhappy moments. It's just that we somehow learn to tolerate such feelings and even start to believe they are 'natural'. We might even go to the horror movie, have feelings of fear invoked, and then call it happiness when we tell others about how great the movie was!

 The coaching questions for self-reflection: "What am I attached to which I believe is giving me happiness? Make a list. Then ask your self if you are sure they make you happy and could you be happy without them. If not why not?

Toxic Belief No 6
Happiness is Relief from Pain or Suffering

Perhaps the most common confusion around happiness is when some pain or suffering ends and we say, "I am so happy the pain has gone." However pain relief can never be authentic happiness, only a temporary relief from unhappiness. Authentic happiness is only possible when we are able to accept the inevitability of physical pain and when we have realized and applied the wisdom to not create any more suffering. Pain is physical, which is why it will inevitably happen at some stage. But suffering is mental and emotional which is always entirely our own creation. It's just that we find it hard to see through the mists of the primary illusion that other people are responsible for our feelings. When we do, it marks the beginning of the end of our 'suffering', which is, in effect, the ending of unhappiness.

 The coaching questions for self-reflection: "What forms of pain am I looking forward to ending so that I can be happy?" Is there a list? Can you decide to accept the pain here in this moment now? Can you discern how you make your self suffer? Describe it!

Toxic Belief No 7
Happiness is only Possible when there is Success

Brilliantly conditioned to believe that the world and life is innately competitive, many of us then form the belief that success equals winning. That could, and usually does, include winning our survival! So we live in fear of losing, fear of not surviving, which creates many unhappy moments. Then we start to compare our successfulness against others' successes, inducing more unhappy moments!

Trying to be more successful today than yesterday, aspiring to be more successful than others, is what turns life into an ultra serious journey, a joyless expedition, a discontented sojourn. You only have to look at the faces of our so called sporting heroes as they participate in their games in the name of 'success' to see the total absence of a natural and authentic happiness. Yet we believe that their success brings them so much happiness! Then we start to believe that the pain of all the strain is the only way to success and therefore happiness. So we start to make ourselves extremely unhappy in order to be happy!

You can only laugh...when you see it in this light!

 The coaching questions for self-reflection: "What kind of successes am I striving towards in the belief they will bring me happiness?" Make a list. Then ask your self if you are sure they will bring you real, authentic, natural happiness. If not why not?

There are probably many more than seven toxic beliefs contaminating our consciousness and sabotaging our natural state of contentment, our pure joyfulness, our original bliss. But recognizing them, and realizing how they are inducing feelings of discontentment, joylessness and frequent moments of grumpiness, is the first step in the purification of our consciousness.

Just as we value pure water over contaminated water, so the spiritual process of the purification of our consciousness includes the elimination of the viral and toxic beliefs that have been absorbed along the way.

The questions provide reflective signposts that you can use to deepen your awareness and invoke your own realizations. However, equally necessary is time spent in that deeper state of consciousness. It's in moments of meditation that it's possible to touch and taste our original and unpolluted state of being. The more you do the easier it becomes to recognize, extract and eliminate anything that pollutes that state.

Be well, stay well, go well...
...and thanks for reading!

The Immune System of the SOUL
Make Your Diagnosis Part I

This is an awareness exercise that allows you to see which form of dis – ease that you 'insperience' most and then what you need to realise to return to a state of ease!

Dis- Ease	Thoughts	Emotions	Behaviour	Viral Belief (The Cause)	The Truth (The Cure)
Paralysis	"Something terrible is about to happen…" "I am sure this is going to end badly…"	*Fear and its variations (in this case it's 'worry')*	Defensive Aggressive Protective	I am 'about' to lose something or someone that I value	**Nothing 'real' can ever be lost because nothing is ever 'mine'**
Crippled		A			
Allergy					
Incontinence					
Indigestion					

Marry the symptoms below to the Dis – Ease on the opposite page

The Thoughts are in inverted commas – The Emotions are in Italics – The Truth is in bold

A	B	C	D	E
Sorrow Frustration Apprehension (the matrix of emotion)	*Fear of missing out Excitement Exhaustion*	If I don't keep up with the latest I may miss something important	"I need to tell them…" "Wait till I tell …" "They'll never believe…"	Avoidance Aggressive Controlling

F	G	H	J	K
Talking Telling Stories Unable to listen	"I've let them down…" "What a terrible mistake I have made.." I should not have said that/ done that…	I need to be affirmed as someone 'in the know' and therefore as an 'important person' in other's lives	Apologetic Grovelling Hiding	*Contempt Excitement Outrage*

L	M	N	O	P
Everyone creates a different personality	*Revulsion Irritation Deflation*	I have done something very wrong, therefore I am a bad person	**I am neither good nor bad I am just … me!**	**Nothing is more important than anything else in the world 'out there'**

Q	R	S	T	V
I am OK as 'I am' and don't need to be recognised by others	I can never accept 'them' and get on with them They should be more like me!	Always consuming information and stories about others	"Oh no not them again…" "I just can't stand that person…"	"I wonder what's happening…" "Need to know what's going on…"

The Immune System of the SOUL
Make Your Diagnosis Part II

Dis- Ease	Thoughts	Emotions	Behaviour	Viral Belief (The Cause)	The Truth (That Cures)
Blindness	How dare you..." "That belongs to me..." "I own that..."	*Variations of sadness, anger and fear.*	Reactive Crying Hiding	It's human nature to be attached to things, people, places etc.	Attachment is the underlying cause of all Dis-Ease
Heart Disease					
Insanity					
Diabetes					A
Arthritis					

The Symptoms - Marry the symptoms below to the Dis – Ease on the opposite page

The Thoughts are in inverted commas – The Emotions are in Italics – The Truth is in bold

A	B	C	D	E
I am honoured to be in receipt of their affection and appreciation	Others should do what I say Other people are responsible for my happiness	"They really don't know what they are doing..." "I know more and better..."	"Rigid Stuck Inflexible ..."	Things and people can be possessed and therefore owned and therefore lost

F	G	H	J	K
Blocking Denying Suspicious Embaressed	*Irritation Frustration Sometimes anger Underlying fear*	"I have just lost..." "What a terrible loss..."	I don't deserve such love and kindness	*Mild Anxiety Apprehension*

L	M	N	O	P
Nothing 'real' is ever lost because nothing is ever mine	I am right and always know best	"They should never have done that..." "They should be punished for that..." "You must..."	*Sadness Sorrow and it's variations*	Shouting Ignoring Criticising Attacking Sulking

Q	R	S	T	V
There are many ways to see things and many ways to get a good result	Mourning Sulking Crying	"I'm sure they don't mean it..." "They must want something..."	*Anger and it's many variations*	**I can not control anyone, ever! I am totally responsible for my happiness**

Thanks and Links

Thanks to Manda and 'the greatest team on earth' at the Global Retreat Centre for the silent space to 'see' in the most powerful place to go deep and 'be deep' in the company of the deepest souls.

wwwglobalretreatcentre.com

Thanks to Lucinda for the kind of music which seeps into your heart and nourishes the soul. 'The angel' amidst a hundred thousand - silence becomes YOU!
Thanks to Andy for the ever present smile that embraces the hearts of all who see. You bring such a beautiful note to this world.

www.blissfulmusic.com

Thanks to Marneta for showing us all how to reach the hearts of the children of the world. Now it's time for all the world to be in touch with the heart of Marneta! Yes?

www. relaxkids. com

Thanks to the Brahma Kumaris World Spiritual University where anyone can receive free tuition in meditation and begin their spiritual journey in thousands of centres across throughout 90 countries. But remember, in order to 'know' you may have to stop believing!

www. bkwsu. org

For more of Mike's insights, workshops, retreats, seminars, talks, articles and meditations please see

www.relax7. com

www.mythsoflove.com

www.immunesystemofthesoul.com

About the Author

Mike George 'plays' a variety of roles including author, spiritual teacher, coach, management tutor, mentor, facilitator.

He travels extensively bringing together the three key strands of 21 st century - emotional/spiritual intelligence, leadership development and continuous unlearning. In a unique blend of insight, wisdom and humour Mike entertains as he enlightens, speaks to your heart as he stay's out of your head and points to 'the way' as he waves you off on your journey!

His previous books include:

The 7 Myths About Love...Actually

Don't Get MAD Get Wise

The 7 AHA!s of Highly Enlightened Souls

In the Light of Meditation

Learn to Find Inner Peace

Learn to Relax

1001 Meditations

1001 Ways to Relax

Each year he leads regular awareness and enlightenment retreats across the world including Africa, Australia, Argentina, Brazil, Chile, Croatia, Germany, Italy, Mexico, Scandinavia, Spain and throughout the UK and USA

Mike can be contacted at mike@relax7.com and a schedule of his seminars and talks can usually be found at www.relax7.com

If you would like to receive Mike's regular e-article entitled Clear Thinking you can subscribe at www.relax7.com - it's free.

CPSIA information can be obtained at www.ICGtesting.com
Printed in the USA
BVOW010510090713

324915BV00006B/14/P